BIBLE, CHURCH, TRADITION:
AN EASTERN ORTHODOX VIEW

BIBLE, CHURCH, TRADITION: AN EASTERN ORTHODOX VIEW

VOLUME ONE
in the Collected Works
of
GEORGES FLOROVSKY
Emeritus Professor of Eastern Church History
Harvard University

NORDLAND PUBLISHING COMPANY
BELMONT, MASSACHUSETTS 02178

MAJOR WORKS BY GEORGES FLOROVSKY

The Eastern Fathers of the Fourth Century (in Russian)
The Byzantine Fathers from the Fifth to the Eighth Century (in Russian)
The Ways of Russian Theology (in Russian)

SECOND PRINTING

Library of Congress Catalog Card Number 72-89502
ISBN 913124-02-8
© Copyright 1972 by NORDLAND PUBLISHING COMPANY

PRINTED IN THE UNITED STATES OF AMERICA

About the Author

Born in Odessa in 1893, Father Georges Florovsky was Assistant Professor at the University of Odessa in 1919. Having left Russia, Fr. Florovsky taught philosophy in Prague from 1922 until 1926. He was then invited to the chair of Patrology at St. Sergius' Orthodox Theological Institute in Paris.

In 1948 Fr. Florovsky came to the United States. He was Professor and Dean of St. Vladimir's Theological School until 1955, while also teaching as Adjunct Professor at Columbia University and Union Theological Seminary.

From 1956 until 1964 Fr. Florovsky held the chair of Eastern Church History at Harvard University. Since 1964 he has taught Slavic studies and history at Princeton University.

Fr. Georges Florovsky, *Emeritus Professor of Eastern Church History* at Harvard University and recipient of numerous honorary degrees, is a member of the American Academy of Arts and Sciences.

About the *Collected Works of Fr. Florovsky*

The *Collected Works* of Fr. Georges Florovsky will be published in English and will contain his articles in Slavic studies as well as in Church History and Theology which have previously appeared in Russian, German, French, Bulgarian, Czech, Serbian, Swedish and English. Each volume will be arranged thematically. Included in the *Collected Works* will be his two major works on the Church Fathers (*The Eastern Fathers of the Fourth Century* and *The Byzantine Fathers from the Fifth to the Eighth Century*).

Table of Contents

Council — Christ: The Criterion of Truth — The Meaning of the Appeal to the Fathers

Chapter VII

Following the Fathers — The Mind of the Fathers — The Existential Character of Patristic Theology — The Meaning of the "Age" of the Fathers — The Legacy of Byzantine Theology — St. Gregory Palamas and *Theosis*

CHAPTER I

The Lost Scriptural Mind

"As the Truth is in Jesus" (Ephesians 4:21)

CHRISTIAN MINISTERS are not supposed to preach their private opinions, at least from the pulpit. Ministers are commissioned and ordained in the church precisely to preach the Word of God. They are given some fixed terms of reference—namely, the gospel of Jesus Christ—and they are committed to this sole and perennial message. They are expected to propagate and to sustain "the faith which was once delivered unto the saints." Of course, the Word of God must be preached "efficiently." That is, it should always be so presented as to carry conviction and command the allegiance of every new generation and every particular group. It may be restated in new categories, if the circumstances require. But, above all, the identity of the message must be preserved.

One has to be sure that one is preaching the same gospel that was delivered and that one is not introducing instead any "strange gospel" of his own. The Word of God cannot be easily adjusted or accommodated to the fleeting customs and attitudes of any particular age, including our own time. Unfortunately, we are often inclined to measure the Word of God by our own stature, instead of checking our mind by the stature of Christ. The "modern mind" also stands under the judgment of the Word of God.

Modern Man and Scripture

But it is precisely at this point that our major difficulty begins. Most of us have lost the integrity of the scriptural mind, even if some bits of biblical phraseology are retained. The modern man often complains that the truth of God is offered to him in an "archaic idiom"—i.e., in the language of the Bible—which is no more his own and cannot be used spontaneously. It has recently been suggested that we should radically "demythologize" Scripture, meaning to replace the antiquated categories of the Holy Writ by something more modern. Yet the question cannot be evaded: Is the language of Scripture really nothing else than an accidental and external wrapping out of which some "eternal idea" is to be extricated and disentangled, or is it rather a perennial vehicle of the divine message, which was once delivered for all time?

We are in danger of losing the uniqueness of the Word of God in the process of continuous "reinterpretation." But how can we interpret at all if we have forgotten the original language? Would it not be safer to bend our thought to the mental habits of the biblical language and to relearn the idiom of the Bible? No man can receive the gospel unless he repents—"changes his mind." For in the language of the gospel "repentance" *(metanoeite)* does not mean merely acknowledgment of and contrition for sins, but precisely a "change of mind"—a profound change of man's mental and emotional attitude, an integral renewal of man's self, which begins in his self-renunciation and is accomplished and sealed by the Spirit.

We are living now in an age of intellectual chaos and disintegration. Possibly modern man has not yet made up his mind, and the variety of opinions is beyond any hope of reconciliation. Probably the only luminous signpost we have to guide us through the mental fog of our desperate age is just the "faith which was once delivered unto the saints," obsolete or archaic as the idiom of the early church may seem to be, judged by our fleeting standards.

Preach the Creeds!

What, then, are we going to preach? What would I preach to my contemporaries "in a time such as this"? There is no room for hesitation: I am going to preach Jesus, and him crucified and risen. I am going to preach and to commend to all whom I may be called to address the message of salvation, as it has been handed down to me by an uninterrupted tradition of the Church Universal. I would not isolate myself in my own age. In other words, I am going to preach the "doctrines of the creed."

I am fully aware that creeds are a stumbling block for many in our own generation. "The creeds are venerable symbols, like the tattered flags upon the walls of national churches; but for the present warfare of the church in Asia, in Africa, in Europe and America the creeds, when they are understood, are about as serviceable as a battle-ax or an arquebus in the hands of a modern soldier." This was written some years ago by a prominent British scholar who is a devout minister too. Possibly he would not write them today. But there are still many who would wholeheartedly make this vigorous statement their own. Let us remember, however, that the early creeds were deliberately scriptural, and it is precisely their scriptural phraseology that makes them difficult for the modern man.

Thus we face the same problem again: What can we offer instead of Holy Scripture? I would prefer the language of the Tradition, not because of a lazy and credulous "conservatism" or a blind "obedience" to some external "authorities," but simply because I cannot find any better phraseology. I am prepared to expose myself to the inevitable charge of being "antiquarian" and "fundamentalist." And I would protest that such a charge is gratuitous and wrong. I do keep and hold the "doctrines of the creed," conscientiously and wholeheartedly, because I apprehend by faith their perennial adequacy and relevance to all ages and to all situations, including "a time such as this." And I believe it is precisely the "doctrines of the creed" that can enable a desperate generation like ours to regain Christian courage and vision.

The Tradition Lives

"The church is neither a museum of dead deposits nor a society of research." The deposits are alive—*depositum juvenescens,* to use the phrase of St. Irenaeus. The creed is not a relic of the past, but rather the "sword of the Spirit." The reconversion of the world to Christianity is what we have to preach in our day. This is the only way out of that impasse into which the world has been driven by the failure of Christians to be truly Christian. Obviously, Christian doctrine does not answer *directly* any practical question in the field of politics or economics. Neither does the gospel of Christ. Yet its impact on the whole course of human history has been enormous. The recognition of human dignity, mercy and justice roots in the gospel. The new world can be built only by a new man.

What Chalcedon Meant

"And was made man." What is the ultimate connotation of this creedal statement? Or, in other words, *who* was Jesus, the Christ and the Lord? What does it mean, in the language of the Council of Chalcedon, that the same Jesus was "perfect man" and "perfect God," yet a single and unique personality? "Modern man" is usually very critical of that definition of Chalcedon. It fails to convey any meaning to him. The "imagery" of the creed is for him nothing more than a piece of poetry, if anything at all. The whole approach, I think, is wrong. The "definition" of Chalcedon is not a metaphysical statement, and was never meant to be treated as such. Nor was the mystery of the Incarnation just a "metaphysical miracle." The formula of Chalcedon was a statement of faith, and therefore cannot be understood when taken out of the total experience of the church. In fact, it is an "existential statement."

Chalcedon's formula is, as it were, an intellectual contour of the mystery which is apprehended by faith. Our Redeemer is *not* a man, but God *himself*. Here lies the existential emphasis of the statement. Our Redeemer is one who "came down" and who, by "being made man," identified himself with men in the fellowship of a truly human life and nature. Not only the initiative was divine, but the Captain of Salvation was a divine Person. The fullness of the human nature of Christ means simply the adequacy and truth of this redeeming identification. God enters human history and becomes a historical person.

This sounds paradoxical. Indeed there is a mystery: "And without controversy great is the mystery of godliness; God was manifested in the flesh." But this mystery was a revelation; the true character of God had been disclosed in the Incarnation. God was so much and so intimately concerned with the destiny of man (and precisely with the destiny of every one of "the little ones") as to intervene *in person* in the chaos and misery of the lost life. The divine providence therefore is not merely an omnipotent ruling of the universe from an august distance by the divine majesty, but a kenosis, a "self-humiliation" of the God of glory. There is a *personal* relationship between God and man.

Tragedy in a New Light

The whole of the human tragedy appears therefore in a new light. The mystery of the Incarnation was a mystery of the love divine, of the divine identification with lost man. And the climax of Incarnation was the cross. It is the turning point of human destiny. But the awful mystery of the cross is comprehensible only in the wider perspective of an integral Christology; that is, only if we believe that the Crucified was in very truth "the Son of the living God." The death of Christ was God's entrance into the misery of human death (again *in person*), a descent into Hades, and this meant the end of death and the inauguration of life everlasting for man.

There is an amazing coherence in the body of the traditional doctrine. But it can be apprehended and understood only in the living context of faith, by which I mean in a personal communion with the personal God. Faith alone makes formulas convincing; faith alone makes formulas live. "It seems paradoxical, yet it is the experience of all observers of spiritual things: no one profits by the Gospels unless he be first in love with Christ." For Christ is not a text but a living Person, and he abides in his body, the church.

A New Nestorianism

It may seem ridiculous to suggest that one should preach the doctrine of Chalcedon "in a time such as this." Yet it is precisely this doctrine—that reality to which this doctrine bears witness—that can change the whole spiritual outlook of modern man. It brings him a true freedom. Man is not alone in this world, and God is taking personal interest in the events of human history. This is an immediate implication of the integral conception of the Incarnation. It is an illusion that the Christological disputes of the past are irrelevant to the contemporary situation. In fact, they are continued and repeated in the controversies of our own age. Modern man, deliberately or subconsciously, is tempted by the Nestorian extreme. That is to say, he does not take the Incarnation in earnest. He does not dare to believe that Christ is a divine person. He wants to have a *human* redeemer, only assisted by God. He is more interested in the human psychology of the Redeemer than in the mystery of the divine love. Because, in the last resort, he believes optimistically in the dignity of man.

A New Monophysitism

On the other extreme we have in our days a revival of "monophysite" tendencies in theology and religion, when man is reduced to complete passivity and is allowed only to listen and to hope. The present tension between "liberalism" and "neo-orthodoxy" is in fact a re-enactment of the old Christological struggle, on a new existential level and in a new spiritual key. The conflict will never be settled or solved in the field of theology, unless a wider vision is acquired.

In the early church the preaching was emphatically theological. It was not a vain speculation. The New Testament itself is a theological book. Neglect of theology in the instruction given to laity in modern times is responsible both for the decay of personal religion and for that sense of frustration which dominates the modern mood. What we need in Christendom "in a time such as this" is precisely a sound and existential theology. In fact, both clergy and the laity are hungry for theology. And because no theology is usually preached, they adopt some "strange ideologies" and combine them with the fragments of traditional beliefs. The whole appeal of the "rival gospels" in our days is that they offer some sort of pseudo theology, a system of pseudo dogmas. They are gladly accepted by those who cannot find any theology in the reduced Christianity of "modern" style. That existential alternative which many face in our days has been aptly formulated by an English theologian, "Dogma or ... death." The age of a-dogmatism and pragmatism has closed. And therefore the ministers of the church have to preach again doctrines and dogmas—the Word of God.

The Modern Crisis

The first task of the contemporary preacher is the "reconstruction of belief." It is by no means an intellectual endeavor. Belief is just the map of the true world, and should not be mistaken for reality. Modern man has been too much concerned with his own ideas and convictions, his own attitudes and reactions. The modern crisis precipitated by humanism (an undeniable fact) has been brought about by the rediscovery of the real world, in which we do believe. The rediscovery of the church is the most decisive aspect of this new spiritual realism. Reality is no more screened from us by the wall of our own ideas. It is again accessible. It is again realized that the church is not just a company of believers, but the "Body of Christ." This is a rediscovery of a new dimension, a rediscovery of the continuing presence of the divine Redeemer in the midst of his faithful flock. This discovery throws a new flood of light on the misery of our disintegrated existence in a world thoroughly secularized. It is already recognized by many that the true solution of all social problems lies somehow in the reconstruction of the church. "In a time such as this" one has to preach the "whole Christ," Christ and the church—*totus Christus, caput et corpus,* to use the famous phrase of St. Augustine. Possibly this preaching is still unusual, but it seems to be the only way to preach the Word of God efficiently in a period of doom and despair like ours.

The Relevance of the Fathers

I have often a strange feeling. When I read the ancient classics of Christian theology, the fathers of the church, I find them more relevant to the troubles and problems of my own time than the production of modern theologians. The fathers were wrestling with existential problems, with those revelations of the eternal issues which were described and recorded in Holy Scripture. I would risk a suggestion that St. Athanasius and St. Augustine are much more up to date than many of our theological contemporaries. The reason is very simple: they were dealing with things and not with the maps, they were concerned not so much with what man can believe as with what God had done for man. We have, "in a time such as this," to enlarge our perspective, to acknowledge the masters of old, and to attempt for our own age an existential synthesis of Christian experience.

CHAPTER II

Revelation and Interpretation

*For what if some did not believe? Shall their
unbelief make the faith of God without effect?*
(Rom. 3:3)

Message and witness

What is the Bible? Is it a book like any other intended for any occasional reader, who is expected to grasp at once its proper meaning? Rather, it is a *sacred* book addressed primarily to believers. Of course, a sacred book can be read by anyone as well, just "as literature." But this is rather irrelevant to our immediate purpose. We are concerned now not with the letter but with the message. St. Hilary put it emphatically: *Scriptura est non in legendo, sed in intelligendo.* [Scripture is not in the reading, but in the understanding.] Is there any definite message in the Bible, taken as a whole, as one book? And again, to whom is this message, if any, properly addressed? To individuals, who would be, as such, entitled to understand the book and to expound its message? Or to the community, and to individuals only in so far as they are members of that community?

Whatever the origin of particular documents included in the book may have been, it is obvious that the book, as a

---

"Revelation and Interpretation" appeared in *Biblical Authority for Today,* edited by A. Richardson and W. Schweitzer (London & Philadelphia, 1951), pp. 163—180.

whole, was a creation of the community, both in the old dispensation and in the Christian Church. The Bible is by no means a complete *collection* of all historical, legislative and devotional writings available, but a *selection* of some, authorized and authenticated by the use (first of all liturgical) in the community, and finally by the formal authority of the Church. And there was some very definite purpose by which this "selection" was guided and checked. "And many other signs truly did Jesus in the presence of his disciples, which are not written in this book. But these are written, that ye might believe that Jesus is the Christ, the Son of God; and that believing ye might have life through his name" (John 20.30-31). The same applies, more or less, to the whole Bible. Certain writings have been selected, edited and compiled, and brought together, and then commended to believers, to the people, as an authorized version of the divine message. The message is divine; it comes from God; it is the Word of God. But it is the faithful community that acknowledges the Word spoken and testifies to its truth. The sacred character of the Bible is ascertained by faith. The Bible, as a book, has been composed in the community and was meant primarily for its edification. The book and the Church cannot be separated. The book and the Covenant belong together, and Covenant implies people. It was the People of the Covenant to whom the Word of God had been entrusted under the old dispensation (Rom. 3.2), and it is the Church of the Word Incarnate that keeps the message of the Kingdom. The Bible is the Word of God indeed, but the book stands by the testimony of the Church. The canon of the Bible is obviously established and authorized by the Church.

One has, however, not to overlook the missionary background of the New Testament. "The Apostolic Preaching," therein embodied and recorded, had a double purpose: the edification of the faithful and the conversion of the world. Therefore the New Testament is not a community-book in the same exclusive sense as the Old Testament surely was. It is still a *missionary* book. Yet it is no less fenced-off from the outsiders. Tertullian's attitude to the Scriptures was typical. He was not prepared to discuss the controversial topics of the faith with heretics on the Scriptural ground. Scriptures belonged to the Church. Heretics' appeal to them was unlawful. They had no right on foreign property. Such was his main argument in the famous treatise: *De praescriptione haereticorum.* An unbeliever has no access to the message, simply because he does not "receive" it. For him there is no "message" in the Bible.

It was no accident that a diverse anthology of writings, composed at various dates and by various writers, came to be regarded as a single book. *Ta biblia* is of course plural but *the Bible* is emphatically singular. The scriptures are indeed one Holy Scripture, one Holy Writ. There is one main theme and one main message through the whole story. For there is a story. Or, even more, the Bible itself is this story, the story of God's dealings with his chosen people. The Bible records first of all God's acts and mighty deeds, *Magnalia Dei.* The process has been initiated by God. There is a beginning and an end, which is also a goal. There is a starting point: the original divine *fiat*—"in the beginning" (Gen. 1.1). And there will be an end: "even so come" (Rev. 22.20). There is one composite and yet single story—from Genesis to Revelation. And this story is history. There is a process going on between these two terminal points. And this process has a definite direction. There is an ultimate goal, an ultimate consummation is expected. Every particular moment is correlated to both terms and has thereby its proper and unique place within the whole. No moment therefore can be understood except in the whole context and perspective.

God has spoken "at sundry times and in divers manners" (Heb. 1.1). He was revealing himself through ages, not once, but constantly, again and again. He was leading his people from truth to truth. There were stages in his revelation: *per incrementa.* This diversity and variety should not be ignored or overlooked. Yet it was ever the same God, and his ultimate message was ever the same. It is the identity of this message that gives to the various writings their real unity, despite the variety of manners. Different versions were taken into the book as they stood. The Church has resisted all attempts to substitute a single synthetic Gospel for four differing Gospels, to transform the *Tetraevangelion* into a *Dia-tessaron,* in spite of the difficulties implied in the "contradictions of the Evangelists" (with which St. Augustine was wrestling). These four Gospels did secure the unity of the message well enough, and perhaps in a more concrete form than any other compilation could afford.

The Bible is a book about God. But the God of the Bible is not *Deus absconditus,* but *Deus revelatus.* God is manifesting and revealing himself. God intervenes in human life. And the Bible is not merely a human record of these divine interventions and deeds. It is a kind of divine intervention itself. It carries with itself a divine message. God's deeds constitute themselves a message. No need therefore to escape time or history in order to meet God. For God is meeting man in history, i.e. in the human element, in the midst of man's daily existence. History belongs to God, and God enters human history. The Bible is intrinsically historical: it is a record of the divine acts, not so much a presentation of God's eternal mysteries, and these mysteries themselves are available only by a historical mediation. "No man hath seen God at any time; the only begotten Son, which is in the bosom of the Father, he hath declared him" (John 1.18). And he declared him by entering history, in his holy incarnation. Thus the historical frame of the revelation is not something that ought to be done away with. There is no need to abstract revealed truth from the frame in which revelations took place. On the contrary, such an abstraction would have abolished the truth as well. For the Truth is not an idea, but a person, even the Incarnate Lord.

In the Bible we are struck by the intimate relation of God to man and of man to God. It is an intimacy of the Covenant, an intimacy of election and adoption. And this intimacy culminates in the incarnation. "God sent forth his Son, born of a woman, born under the law" (Gal. 4.4). In the Bible we see not only God, but man too. It is the revelation of God, but what is actually revealed is God's concern about man. God reveals himself to man, "appears" before him, "speaks" and converses with him so as to reveal to man the hidden meaning of his own existence and the ultimate purpose of his life. In Scripture we see God coming to reveal himself to man, and we see man meeting God, and not only listening to his voice, but answering him too. We hear in the Bible not only the voice of God, but also the voice of man answering him—in words of prayer, thanksgiving and adoration, awe and love, sorrow and contrition, exultation, hope or despair. There are, a sit were, two partners in the Covenant, God and man, and both belong together, in the mystery of the true divine-human encounter, which is described and recorded in the story of the Covenant. Human response is integrated into the mystery of the Word of God. It is not a divine monologue, it is rather a dialogue, and both are speaking, God and man. But prayers and invocations of the worshipping psalmist are nevertheless "the Word of God." God wants, and expects, and demands this answer and response of man. It is for this that he reveals himself to man and speaks to him. He is, as it were, waiting for man to converse with him. He establishes his Covenant with the sons of men. Yet, all this intimacy does not compromise divine sovereignty and transcendence. God is "dwelling in light unapproachable" (I Tim. 6.16). This light, however, "lighteth every man that cometh into the world" (John 1.9). This constitutes the mystery, or the "paradox" of the revelation.

Revelation is the history of the Covenant. Recorded revelation, i.e. the Holy Scripture, is therefore, above all, history. Law and prophets, psalms and prophecies, all are included and, as it were, woven into the living historical web. Revelation is not a system of divine oracles only. It is primarily the system of divine deeds; one might say, revelation was the path of God in history. And the climax was reached when God entered history himself, and for ever: when the Word of God was incarnate and "made man." On the other hand, the book of revelation is as well the book of human destiny. First of all, it is a book which narrates the creation, fall and salvation of man. It is the story of salvation, and therefore man organically belongs to the story. It shows us man in his obedience and in his obstinate rebellion, in his fall and in his restoration. And the whole human fate is condensed and exemplified in the destiny of Israel, old and new, the chosen people of God, a people for God's own possession. The fact of election is here of basic importance. One people has been elected, set apart from all other nations, constituted as a sacred oasis in the midst of human disorder. With one people on earth only did God establish his Covenant and grant his own sacred law. Here only a true priesthood has been created, even though but a provisional one. In this nation only true prophets were raised, who spoke words inspired by the Spirit of God. It was a sacred, though hidden centre for the whole world, an oasis granted by God's mercy, in the midst of a fallen, sinful, lost and unredeemed world. All this is not the letter, but the very heart of the Biblical message. And all this came from God, there was no human merit or achievement. Yet, all this came for the sake of man, "for us men and for our salvation." All these privileges granted to the Israel of old were subordinate to the ultimate purpose, that of a universal salvation: "For salvation is of the Jews" (John 4.22). The redeeming purpose is ever universal indeed, but it is being accomplished always by means of separation, selection or setting apart. In the midst of human fall and ruin a sacred oasis is erected by God. The Church is also an oasis still, set apart, though not taken out of the world. For again this oasis is not a refuge or shelter only, but rather a citadel, a vanguard of God.

There is a centre in the Biblical story, or a crucial point on the line of the temporal events. There is a new beginning within the process, which does not, however, divide or cut it into parts, but rather gives to it an ultimate cohesion and unity. The distinction between the two Testaments belongs itself to the unity of the Biblical revelation. The two Testaments are to be carefully distinguished, never to be confused. Yet they are organically linked together, not as two systems only, but primarily in the person of the Christ. Jesus the Christ belongs to both. He is the fulfiller of the old dispensation and by the same act that he fulfills the old, "the Law and the prophets," he inaugurates the new, and thereby becomes the ultimate fulfiller of both, i.e. of the whole. He is the very centre of the Bible, just because he is the *archē* and the *telos*—the beginning and the end. And unexpectedly this mysterious identity of the start, the centre and the goal, instead of destroying the existential reality of time, gives to the time-process its genuine reality and full meaning. There are no mere happenings which pass by, but rather events and achievements, and new things are coming to existence, that which never existed before. "Behold I make all things new" (Rev. 21.5).

Ultimately, the Old Testament as a whole has to be considered as "a book of the generation of Jesus Christ, the Son of David, the Son of Abraham" (Matt. 1.1). It was the period of promises and expectation, the time of covenants and prophecies. It was not only the prophets that prophesied. Events also were prophecies. The whole story was prophetical or "typical," a prophetical sign hinting forward towards approaching consummation. Now, the time of expectation is over. The promise had been accomplished. The Lord has come. And he came to abide among his people for ever. The history of flesh and blood is closed. The history of the Spirit is disclosed: "Grace and truth came by Jesus Christ" (John 1.17). But it was an accomplishment, not destruction of the old. *Vetus Testamentum in Novo patet.* [The Old Testament extends into the New]. And *patet* means precisely: is revealed, disclosed, fulfilled. Therefore, the books of the Hebrews are still sacred, even for the new Israel of Christ— not to be left out or ignored. They tell us still the story of salvation, *Magnalia Dei.* They do still bear witness to Christ. They are to be read in the Church as a book of sacred history, not to be transformed into a collection of proof-texts or of theological instances *(loci theologici),* nor into a book of parables. Prophecy has been accomplished and law has been superseded by grace. But nothing has passed away. In sacred history, "the past" does not mean simply "passed" or "what had been," but primarily that which had been accomplished and fulfilled. "Fulfilment" is the basic category of revelation. That which has become sacred remains consecrated and holy for ever. It has the seal of the Spirit. And the Spirit breathes still in the words once inspired by him. It is true, perhaps, that in the Church and for us now the Old Testament is no more than a book, simply because the Law and the Prophets were superseded by the Gospel. The New Testament is obviously more than a book. We do belong to the New Testament ourselves. We are the People of the New Covenant. For that reason it is precisely in the Old Testament that we apprehend revelation primarily as the Word: we witness to the Spirit "that spake through the prophets." For in the New Testament God has spoken by his Son, and we are called upon not only to listen, but to look at. "That which we have seen and heard declare we unto you" (I John 1.3). And, furthermore, we are called upon to *be* "in Christ."

The fullness of revelation is Christ Jesus. And the New Testament is history no less than the Old: the Gospel history of the Incarnate Word and the beginnings of church history, and the apocalyptic prophecy too. The Gospel is history. *Historic events* are the source and the basis of all Christian faith and hope. The basis of the New Testament is facts, events, deeds—not only teaching, commandments or words. From the very beginning, from the very day of Pentecost, when St. Peter as an eye-witness (Acts 2.32: "whereof we are all witnesses," *martyres*) witnessed to the fulfilment of salvation in the Risen Lord, apostolic preaching had emphatically an historical character. By this historical witness the Church stands. Creeds have an historical structure too, they refer to the events. Again, it is a sacred history. The mystery of Christ is precisely in that "in him dwelleth all the fulness of the Godhead bodily" (Col. 2.9). This mystery cannot be comprehended within the earthly plane alone, there is another dimension too. But historical boundaries are not obliterated, not dimmed: in the sacred image historical features are clearly seen. Apostolic preaching was always a narrative, a narrative of what had really happened, *hic et nunc*. But what happened was ultimate and new: "The Word was made flesh" (John 1.14). Of course, the Incarnation, the Resurrection, the Ascension are historical facts not quite in the same sense or on the same level as the happenings of our own daily life. But they are no less historical for that, no less factual. On the contrary, they are more historical—they are ultimately eventful. They cannot obviously be fully ascertained except by faith. Yet this does not take them out of the historical context. Faith only discovers a new dimension, apprehends the historical *datum* in its full depth, in its full and ultimate reality. The Evangelists and the Apostles were no chroniclers. It was not their mission to keep the full record of all that Jesus had done, day by day, year by year. They describe his life and relate his works, so as to give us his image: an historic, and yet a divine image. It is no portrait, but rather an *ikon*—but surely an historic *ikon,* an image of the Incarnate Lord. Faith does not create a new value; it only discovers the inherent one. Faith itself is a sort of vision, "the evidence of things not seen" (Heb. 11.1: St. John Chrysostom explains *elenchos* precisely as *opsis*). The "invisible" is no less real than "visible"—rather more real. "And yet no man can say that Jesus is the Lord, but by the Holy Ghost" (I Cor. 12.3). It means that the Gospel itself can be apprehended in all its fulness and depth only in spiritual experience. But what is discovered by faith is given in very truth. The Gospels are written within the church. In this sense they are the witness of the Church. They are records of church experience and faith. But they are no less historical narratives and bear witness to what had really taken place, in space and in time. If "by faith" we discover much more than what can be detected "by senses," this only discloses the utter inadequacy of "senses" in the knowledge of spiritual matters. For what had really happened was the mighty deed of the Redeeming God, his ultimate intervention in the stream of historical events. One should not divorce the "fact" and the "meaning"—both are given in reality.

Revelation is preserved in the Church. Therefore, the Church is the proper and primary interpreter of revelation. It is protected and reinforced by written words; protected, but not exhausted. Human words are no more than signs. The testimony of the Spirit revives the written words. We do not mean now the occasional illumination of individuals by the Holy Ghost, but primarily the permanent assistance of the Spirit given to the Church, that is "the pillar and bulwark of the truth" (I Tim. 3.15). The Scriptures need interpretation. Not the phrasing, but the message is the core. And the Church is the divinely appointed and permanent witness to the very truth and the full meaning of this message, simply because the Church belongs itself to the revelation, as the Body of the Incarnate Lord. The proclamation of the Gospel, the preaching of the Word of God, obviously belongs to the *esse* of the Church. The Church stands by its testimony and witness. But this witness is not just a reference to the past, not merely a reminiscence, but rather a continuous rediscovery of the message once delivered to the saints and ever since kept by faith. Moreover, this message is ever re-enacted in the life of the Church. Christ himself is ever present in the Church, as the Redeemer and head of his Body, and continues his redeeming office in the Church. Salvation is not only announced or proclaimed in the Church. but precisely enacted. The sacred history is still continued. The mighty deeds of God are still being performed. *Magnalia Dei* are not circumscribed by the past; they are ever present and continued, in the Church and, through the Church, in the world. The Church is itself an integral part of the New Testament message. The Church itself is a part of revelation—the story of "the Whole Christ" (*totus Christus: caput et corpus,* in the phrase of St. Augustine) and of the Holy Ghost. The ultimate end of revelation, its *telos,* has not yet come. And only within the experience of the Church is the New Testament truly and fully alive. Church history is itself a story of redemption. The truth of the book is revealed and vindicated by the growth of the Body.

History and System

We must admit at once that the Bible is a difficult book, a book sealed with seven seals. And, as time runs on, it grows no easier. The main reason for that, however, is not that the Book is written in an "unknown tongue" or contains some "secret words that man may not repeat." On the contrary, the very stumbling-block of the Bible is its utter simplicity: the mysteries of God are framed into the daily life of average men, and the whole story may seem to be all too human. Just as the Incarnate Lord himself appeared to be an ordinary man.

The Scriptures are "inspired," they are the Word of God. What is the inspiration can never be properly defined—there is a mystery therein. It is a mystery of the divine-human encounter. We cannot fully understand in what manner "God's holy men" heard the Word of their Lord and how they could articulate it in the words of their own dialect. Yet, even in their human transmission it was the voice of God. Therein lies the miracle and the mystery of the Bible, that it is the Word of God in human idiom. And, in whatever the manner we understand the inspiration, one factor must not be overlooked. The Scriptures transmit and preserve the Word of God precisely in the idiom of man. God spoke to man indeed, but there was man to attend and to perceive. "Anthropomorphism" is thus inherent in the very fact. There is no accommodation to human frailty. The point is rather that the human tongue does not lose its natural features to become a vehicle of divine revelation. If we want the divine word to ring clear, our tongue is not to leave off being human. What is human is not swept away by divine inspiration, it is only *transfigured.* The "supernatural" does not destroy what is "natural": *hyper physin* does not mean *para physin.* The human idiom does not betray or belittle the splendour of revelation, it does not bind the power of God's Word. The Word of God may be adequately and rightly expressed in human words. The Word of God does not grow dim when it sounds in the tongue of man. For man is created in the image and likeness of God—this "analogical" link makes communication possible. And since God deigned to speak to man, the human word itself acquires new depth and strength and becomes transfigured. The divine Spirit breathes in the organism of human speech. Thus it becomes possible for man to utter words of God, to speak of God. "Theology" becomes possible—*theologia,* i.e. *logos peri theou.* Strictly speaking, theology grows possible only through revelation.

It is the human response to God, who has spoken first. It is man's witness to God who has spoken to him, whose word he has heard, whose words he has kept and is now recording and repeating. Surely this response is never complete. Theology is ever in the process of formation. The basis and the starting point are ever the same: the Word of God, the revelation. Theology witnesses back to the revelation. It witnesses in divers manners: in creeds, in dogmas, in sacred rites and symbols. But in a sense Scripture itself is the primary response, or rather Scripture itself is at once both the Word of God and the human response—the Word of God mediated through the faithful response of man. There is always some human interpretation in any Scriptural presentation of the divine Word. So far it is always inescapably "situation-conditioned." Is it ever possible for man to escape his human situation?

The Church has summarized the Scriptural message in creeds, and in many other ways and methods. Christian faith has developed or grown into a system of beliefs and convictions. In any such system the inner structure of the basic message is shown forth, all particular articles of faith are presented in their mutual interdependence. Obviously, we need a system, as we need a map in our travels. But maps refer to a real land. And any doctrinal system too must be related to the revelation. It is of utter importance that the Church has never thought of her dogmatic system as a kind of substitute for the Scriptures. Both are to be kept side by side: a somewhat abstract or generalized presentation of the main message in a creed or in a system, and all particular documents referring to the concrete instances of revelation. One might say a *system* and the *history* itself.

Here a problem arises: how, and to what extent, can history be framed into a system? This is the main problem of theological hermeneutics. What is the *theological* use of the Bible? How should the divers and concrete witnesses, covering hundreds of years, be used for the construction of a single scheme? The Bible is one indeed, and yet it is, in fact, a collection of various writings. We are not entitled to ignore that. The solution depends ultimately upon our conception of history, upon our vision of time. The easiest solution would have been indeed if we could simply overlook or overcome the diversity of times, the duration of the process itself. Such a temptation faced Christianity from an early date. It was at the root of all allegorical interpretations, from Philo and Pseudo-Barnabas to the new revival of allegorism in post-Reformation times. It was a permanent temptation of all mystics. The Bible is regarded as a book of sacred parables, written in a peculiar symbolical language, and the task of exegesis is to detect their hidden meaning, to detect the eternal Word, which happens to have been uttered in divers manners and under divers veils. The historical truth and perspective are irrelevant in this case. Historical concreteness is no more than a pictorial frame, a poetical imagery. One is in search of *eternal* meanings. The whole Bible would be then reconstructed into a book of edifying examples, of glorious symbols, which point out the supertemporal truth. Is not the truth of God ever the same, identical and eternal? In that mood, it is but natural to look in the Old Testament for the evidences of all distinctive Christian beliefs and convictions. Two Testaments are as it were melted into one, super-temporal, and their distinctive marks obliterated. The dangers and shortcomings of such a hermeneutical approach are too obvious to need an extensive refutation. But the only real remedy against this temptation would be the restoration of historical insight. The Bible is *history,* not a system of belief, and should not be used as a *summa theologiae.* At the same time, it is not history of human belief, but the history of the divine revelation. The basic problem remains, however, still unsolved: for what purpose do we need both system and history? By what reason and for what purpose did the Church keep them always together? Again, the easiest answer to this question is the least satisfactory: one may suggest at once that the Scriptures are the only authentic record of the revelation, and everything else is no more than a commentary thereupon. And commentary can never have the same authority as the original record. There is some truth in this suggestion, but the true difficulty we have to face is elsewhere. Why are not the earlier stages of the revelation superseded by the later ones? Why do we still need the law and the prophets even in the new covenant of Christ, and, to a certain extent, on the same level of authority as the Gospels and the rest of the New Testament writings? I mean, as chapters of the same unique book, as it were. For, obviously, they are included in the canon of Scripture, not as historical documents only, not as chapters on the stages of history already passed away. This applies particularly to the Old Testament. "For all the prophets and the law prophesied until John" (Matt. 11.13). Why do we still keep both the law and the prophets, and in what sense? What can be the right use of the Old Testament in the Church of Christ?

First of all, it needs to be an historical use. Yet, again this history is a sacred history—not a history of human convictions and their evolution, but a history of the mighty deeds of God. And these deeds are not disconnected irruptions of God into human life. There was an intimate unity and cohesion. They led and guided the chosen people into God's supreme purpose, unto Christ. Therefore, in a sense, the earlier ones were reflected, as it were, or implied in the later ones. There was a continuity of the divine action, as there was an identity of the goal and purpose as well. This continuity is the basis of what was called the "typological" interpretation. Patristic terminology was at that point rather fluent. Still, there was always a clear distinction between two methods and approaches. "Allegory" was an exegetical method indeed. An allegorist dealt primarily with the texts; he searched out the hidden and ultimate meaning of Scriptural passages, sentences and even particular words, behind and beneath "the letter." On the contrary, "typology" was not an exegesis of the texts themselves, but rather an interpretation of the events. It was an historical, and not merely a philological method. It was the inner correspondence of the events themselves in the two Testaments that had to be detected, established and brought forward. A typologist looked not for the "parallels" or similarities. And not every event of the Old Testament has its "correspondence" in the New. Yet there are certain basic events in the old dispensation which were the "figures" or "types" of the basic events in the new. Their "correspondence" was of divine appointment: they were, as it were, stages of a single process of the redemptive Providence. In this manner "typology" was practiced already by St. Paul (if under the name of an "allegory": Gal. 4.24: *Hatina estin allegoroumena*). There is an identical purpose of God behind all his mighty interventions, and in full it has been revealed in Christ. St. Augustine put it very clearly: *"in ipso facto, non solum in dicto, mysterium requirere debemus* [We ought to seek the mystery not just in word, but in the fact itself] (*in ps. 68, sermo,* 2, 6). And "the mystery" of the Old Testament was Christ; not only in the sense that Moses or the prophets "spoke" of him, but primarily because the whole stream of sacred history was divinely oriented towards him. And in this sense he was the fulfilment of all prophecies. For that reason, it is only in the light of Christ that the Old Testament can be properly understood and its "mysteries" unveiled—they were, in fact, unveiled by the coming of him "who should come." The true prophetic meaning of the prophecies is clearly seen only, as it were, in retrospect, after they have been actually fulfilled. An unaccomplished prophecy is always dim and enigmatic (so are the prophecies of the Book of Revelation, which point to what is still to come, "at the end"). But it does not mean that we simply put arbitrarily a new meaning into the old text: the meaning was there, though it could not yet be seen clearly. When, for instance, we, in the Church, identify the Suffering Servant (in the Book of Isaiah) as Christ the crucified, we do not simply "apply" an Old Testament vision to a New Testament event: we detect the meaning of the vision itself, although this meaning surely could not have been clearly identified in the times preceding Christ. But what had been first just a vision (i.e. an "anticipation") has becomes an historical fact.

Another point is of utter importance. For an "allegorist" the "images" he interprets are reflections of a pre-existing prototype, or even images of some eternal or abstract "truth." They are pointing to something that is outside of time. On the contrary, typology is oriented towards the future. The "types" are anticipations, *pre*-figurations; their "prototype" is still to come. Typology is thus an historical method, more than a philological one. It presupposes and implies intrinsically the reality of history, directed and guided by God. It is organically connected with the idea of the covenant. Here the past, the present and the future are linked in a unity of divine purpose, and the purpose was Christ. Therefore typology has emphatically a Christological meaning (the Church is included here, as the Body and the Bride of Christ). In practice, of course, a true balance was never strictly kept. Even in patristic use typology was variously contaminated by allegorical deviations or accretions, especially in the devotional and homiletic use. What is, however, of importance is that in the catechetical tradition of the Early Church, closely related to the administration of the sacraments, this balance was always kept. This was the tradition of the Church, and deviations were due more to the curiosity or imagination of individual scholars. The Church was, in full sobriety, historically minded. Along with a presentation of the doctrine (i.e. a system) the Holy Bible was always read in the churches, with the deliberate purpose of reminding the faithful of the historical basis and background of their faith and hope.

St. Augustine suggested that the prophets spoke of the Church even more clearly than of Christ himself, i.e. of the Messiah (*in ps.* 30.2, *enarratio,* 2, M.L., 36, 244). In a sense, this was only natural. For there was already a Church. Israel, the chosen people, the people of the covenant, was much more a Church than a nation, like other "nations." *Ta ethne, nationes* or *gentes*—these kindred terms were used in the Bible (and later) precisely to describe the heathen or pagans in contrast to the only nation or people that was also (and primarily) a Church of God. The Law was given to Israel just in her capacity as a Church. It embraced the whole life of the people, the "temporal" as well as the "spiritual," precisely because the whole of human existence had to be regulated by the divine precepts. And the division of life into "temporal" and "spiritual" departments is, strictly speaking, precarious. In any case, Israel was a divinely constituted community of believers, united by the Law of God, the true faith, sacred rites and hierarchy—we find here all elements of the traditional definition of the Church. The old dispensation has been accomplished in the new, the covenant has been reconstituted, and the old Israel was rejected, because of her utter unbelief: she missed the day of her visitation. The only true continuation of the old covenant was in the Church of Christ (let us remember that both terms are of Hebrew origin: the Church is *qahal* and Christ means *Messiah*). She is the true Israel, *kata pneuma*. In this sense already St. Justin emphatically rejected the idea that the Old Testament was a link holding together the Church and the Synagogue. For him the opposite was true. All Jewish claims were to be formally rejected: the Old Testament no longer belonged to the Jews, as they had not believed in Christ Jesus. The Old Testament belonged now to the Church alone. Nobody could any longer claim Moses and the prophets, if he was not with Jesus the Christ. For the Church was the New Israel and the only heir of the promises of old. A new and important hermeneutical principle was implied in these rigoristic utterances of the early Christian apologist. The Old Testament was to be read and interpreted as a book of the Church. The book *on* the Church, we should add.

The Law was superseded by the truth, and in it has found its accomplishment, and thereby was abrogated. It no longer had to be imposed upon the new converts. The New Israel had its own constitution. This part of the Old Testament was antiquated. It proved to be basically "situation-conditioned"—not so much in the sense of a general historical relativity as in a deeper providential sense. The new redemptive situation had been created or inaugurated by the Lord: a new situation in the sacred perspective of salvation. Everything that belonged essentially to the previous stage or phase had now lost its meaning, or rather kept its meaning as a prefiguration only. Even the Decalogue perhaps was not exempt from this rule and was overruled by the "new commandment." The Old Testament is now to be used solely in its relation to the Church. Under the old dispensation the Church was limited to one nation. In the new all national discriminations are emphatically abrogated: there is no more distinction between a Jew and a Greek—all are indiscriminately in the same Christ. In other words, one has no right to isolate certain elements of the old dispensation, apart from their immediate relation to the life of the Church, and set them as a Scriptural pattern for the temporal life of the nations. The old Israel was a provisional Church, but she was not a pattern nation. One may put it this way. Obviously, we can learn a lot from the Bible on social justice—this was a part of the message of the Kingdom to come. We can learn a lot about a particular political, social and economic organization of the Jews through the ages. All that may possibly be of great help in our sociological discussions. And yet it is hardly permissible to detect in the Bible (viz. in the Old Testament) any permanent or ideal pattern of political or economic settlement for the present or for any other historical realm at all. We may learn quite a lot from Hebrew history. This will, however, be only a historical lesson, not a theological one. Biblical fundamentalism is no better in sociology than anywhere else. The Bible is no authority on social science, as it is no authority on astronomy. The only sociological lesson that can be extracted from the Bible is precisely the fact of the Church, the Body of Christ. But no reference to the Bible in "temporal" affairs can be regarded as a "Scriptural evidence." There are "Scriptural evidences" only in theology. It does not mean that no guidance whatever can be found or even sought there in the Bible. In any case, such a search will not be a "theological use" of the Bible. And perhaps the lessons of the old Hebrew history are on the same level as any other lessons of the past. We have to distinguish more carefully between what was permanent and what was but provisional (or "situation-conditioned") in the old covenant (and first of all we have to overcome its national limitations). Otherwise we would be in danger of overlooking what was new in the new covenant. In the New Testament itself we have to make a clear distinction between its historical and prophetical aspects too. The true theme of the whole Bible is Christ and his Church, not nations or societies, nor the sky and the earth. The old Israel was the "type" of the new, i.e. of the Church Universal, not of any particular or occasional nation. The national frame of the provisional Church has been done away by the universality of salvation. There is, after Christ, but one "nation," the Christian nation, *genus Christianum*—in the ancient phrase, *tertium genus*—i.e. precisely the Church, the only people of God, and no other national description can claim any further Scriptural warrant: national differences belong to the order of nature and are irrelevant in the order of grace.

The Bible is complete. But the sacred history is not yet completed. The Biblical canon itself includes a prophetical Book of Revelation. There is the Kingdom to come, the ultimate consummation, and therefore there are prophecies in the New Testament as well. The whole being of the Church is in a sense prophetical. Yet, the future has a different meaning *post Christum natum*. The tension between present and future has in the Church of Christ another sense and character than it had under the old dispensation. For Christ is no more in the future only, but also in the past, and therefore in the present also. This eschatological perspective is of basic importance for the right understanding of the Scriptures. All hermeneutical "principles" and "rules" should be re-thought and re-examined in this eschatological perspective. There are two major dangers to be avoided. On the one hand, no strict analogy can be established between the two Testaments, their "covenantal situations" being profoundly different: they are related as "the figure" and "the truth." It was a traditional idea of patristic exegesis that the Word of God was revealing himself continuously, and in divers manners, throughout the whole of the Old Testament. Yet all these *theophanies* of old should never be put on the same level or in the same dimension as the incarnation of the Word, lest the crucial event of redemption is dissolved into an allegorical shadow. A "type" is no more than a "shadow" or image. In the New Testament we have the very fact. The New Testament therefore is more than a mere "figure" of the Kingdom to come. It is essentially the realm of accomplishment. On the other hand, it is premature to speak of a "realized eschatology," simply because the very *eschaton* is not yet realized: sacred history has not yet been closed. One may prefer the phrase: "the inaugurated eschatology." It renders accurately the Biblical diagnosis—the crucial point of the revelation is already in the past. "The ultimate" (or "the new") had already entered history, although the final stage is not yet attained. We are no more in the world of signs only, but already in the world of reality, yet under the sign of the Cross. The Kingdom has been already inaugurated, but not yet fulfilled. The fixed canon of Scripture itself symbolizes an accomplishment. The Bible is closed just because the Word of God has been incarnate. Our ultimate term of reference is now not a book, but a living person. Yet the Bible still holds its authority—not only as a record of the past, but also as a prophetical book, full of hints, pointing to the future, to the very end.

The sacred history of redemption is still going on. It is now the history of the Church that is the Body of Christ. The Spirit-Comforter is already abiding in the Church. No complete system of Christian faith is yet possible, for the Church is still on her pilgrimage. And the Bible is kept by the Church as a book of history to remind believers of the dynamic nature of the divine revelation, "at sundry times and in divers manners."

CHAPTER III

The Catholicity of the Church

The Theanthropic Union and the Church

CHRIST conquered the world. This victory consists in His having created His own Church. In the midst of the vanity and poverty, of the weakness and suffering of human history, He laid the foundations of a "new being." The Church is Christ's work on earth; it is the image and abode of His blessed Presence in the world. And on the day of Pentecost the Holy Spirit descended on the Church, which was then represented by the twelve Apostles and those who were with them. He entered into the world in order to abide with us and act more fully than He had ever acted before; "for the Spirit was not yet given, because Jesus was not yet glorified."[1] The Holy Spirit descended once and for always. This is a tremendous and unfathomable mystery. He lives and abides ceaselessly in the Church. In the Church we receive the Spirit of adoption.[2] Through reaching towards and accepting the Holy Ghost we become eternally God's. In the Church our salvation is perfected; the sanctification and transfiguration, the *theosis* of the human race is accomplished.

Extra Ecclesiam nulla salus: [Outside the Church there is no salvation]. All the categorical strength and point of this aphorism lies in its tautology. Outside the Church there is

---

"The Catholicity of the Church" appeared as "Sobornost: The Catholicity of the Church" in *The Church of God*, edited by E. Mascall (London: S.P.C.K., 1934).

no salvation, because *salvation is the Church*. For salvation
is the revelation of the way for every one who believes in
Christ's name. This revelation is to be found only in the
Church. In the Church, as in the Body of Christ, in its theanthropic organism, the mystery of incarnation, the mystery of
the "two natures," indissolubly united, is continually accomplished. In the Incarnation of the Word is the fulness of
revelation, a revelation not only of God, but also of man.
"For the Son of God became the Son of Man," writes St.
Irenaeus, "to the end that man too might become the son
of God."[3] In Christ, as God-Man, the meaning of human
existence is not only revealed, but accomplished. In Christ
human nature is perfected, it is renewed, rebuilt, created
anew. Human destiny reaches its goal, and henceforth human
life is, according to the word of the Apostle, "hid with Christ
in God."[4] In this sense Christ is the "Last Adam,"[5] a true
man. In Him is the measure and limit of human life. He
rose "as the first fruits of them that are asleep,"[6] He ascended
into Heaven, and sitteth at the right hand of God. His Glory
is the glory of all human existence. Christ has entered the
pre-eternal glory; He has entered it as Man and has called
the whole of mankind to abide with Him and in Him. "God,
being rich in mercy, for His great love wherewith He loved
us, even when we were dead through our trespasses, quickened
us together with Christ... and raised us up with Him, and
made us to sit with Him in the heavenly places, in Christ
Jesus."[7] Therein lies the mystery of the Church as Christ's
Body. The Church is fulness, τὸ πλήρωμα that is, *fulfilment,* completion.[8] In this manner St. John Chrysostom explains the words of the Apostle: "The Church is the fulfilment of Christ in the same manner as the head completes
the body and the body is completed by the head. Thus we
understand why the Apostle sees that *Christ,* as the Head.
needs all His members. Because if many of us were not, one
the hand, one the foot, one yet another member, *His body
would not be complete.* Thus His body is formed of all the
members. This means, *that the head will be complete, only
when the body is perfect; when we all are most firmly united
and strengthened.*"[9] Bishop Theophanes repeats the expla-

nation of Chrysostom: "The Church is the fulfilment of Christ in the same manner as the tree is the fulfilment of the grain. All that is contained in the grain in a condensed manner, receives its full development in the tree.... He Himself is complete and all-perfect, but not yet has He drawn mankind to Himself in final completeness. It is only gradually that mankind enters into Communion with Him and so gives a new fulness to His work, which thereby attains its full accomplishment."[10]

The Church is completeness itself; it is the continuation and the fulfilment of the theanthropic union. The Church is transfigured and regenerated mankind. The meaning of this regeneration and transfiguration is that *in the Church mankind becomes one unity,* "in one body."[11] The life of the Church is unity and union. The body is "knit together" and "increaseth"[12] in unity of Spirit, in unity of love. The realm of the Church is unity. And of course this unity is no outward one, but is inner, intimate, organic. It is the unity of the living body, the unity of the organism. The Church is a unity not only in the sense that it is one and unique; it is a unity, first of all, because its very being consists in reuniting separated and divided mankind. *It is this unity which is the "sobornost" or catholicity of the Church.* In the Church humanity passes over into another plane, begins a new manner of existence. A new life becomes possible, a true, whole and complete life, a catholic life, "in the unity of the Spirit, in the bond of peace."[13] A new existence begins, a new principle of life, "even as Thou, Father, art in Me, and I in Thee, that they also may be in Us ... that they may be one even as We are one."[14]

This is the mystery of the final reunion in the image of the Unity of the Holy Trinity. It is realized in the life and construction of the Church, it *is the mystery of sobornost, the mystery of catholicity.*

The Inner Quality of Catholicity

geographical conception. It does not at all depend on the
The catholicity of the Church is not a quantitative or a

world-wide dispersion of the faithful. The universality of the Church is the consequence or the manifestation, but not the cause or the foundation of its catholicity. The world-wide extension or the universality of the Church is only an outward sign, one that is not absolutely necessary. The Church was catholic even when Christian communities were but solitary rare islands in a sea of unbelief and paganism. And the Church will remain catholic even unto the end of time when the mystery of the "falling away" will be revealed, when the Church once more will dwindle to a "small flock." "When the Son of Man cometh, shall He find faith on the earth?"[15] The Metropolitan Philaret expressed himself very adequately on this point: "If a city or a country falls away from the universal Church, the latter will still remain an integral, imperishable body."[16] Philaret uses here the word "universal" in the sense of catholicity. The conception of catholicity cannot be measured by its wide-world expansion; universality does not express it exactly. Καθολική from Καθ' ὅλου means, first of all, the inner wholeness and integrity of the Church's life. We are speaking here of *wholeness,* not only of *communion,* and in any case not of a simple empirical communion. Καθ' ὅλου is not the same as Κατὰ παντός; it belongs not to the phenomenal and empirical, but to the noumenal and ontological plane; it describes the very essence, not the external manifestations. We feel this already in the pre-Christian use of these words, beginning from Socrates. If catholicity also means universality, it certainly is not an empirical universality, but an ideal one; the communion of ideas, not of facts, is what it has in view. The first Christians when using the words 'Εκκλησία Καθολική never meant a world-wide Church. This word rather gave prominence to the orthodoxy of the Church, to the truth of the "Great Church," as contrasted with the spirit of sectarian separatism and particularism; it was the idea of integrity and purity that was expressed. This has been very forcibly stated in the well known words of St. Ignatius of Antioch: "Where there is a bishop, let there be the whole multitude; just as where Jesus Christ is, there too is the Catholic Church."[17] These words express the same idea as does the promise: "Where two or three are gathered together in My name, there am I in the midst of them."[18] It is this mystery of gathering together (μυστήριον τῆς συνάξεως) that the word catholicity expresses. Later on St. Cyril of Jerusalem explained the word "catholicity" which is used in the Creed in the traditional manner of his Church. The word "Church" means the "gathering together of all in one union"; therefore it is called a "gathering" (ἐκκλησία). The Church is called catholic, because it spreads over all the universe and subjects the whole of the human race to righteousness, because also in the Church the dogmas are taught *"fully, without any omission,* catholically, and completely" (καθολικῶς καὶ ἀνελλιπῶς) because, again, in the Church every kind of sin is cured and healed."[19] Here again catholicity is understood as an inner quality. Only in the West, during the struggle against the Donatists was the word "catholica" used in the sense of "universality," in opposition to the geographical provincialism of the Donatists.[20] Later on, in the East, the word "catholic" was understood as synonymous with "ecumenical." But this only limited the conception, making it less vivid, because it drew attention to the outward form, not to the inner contents. Yet the Church is not catholic because of its outward extent, or, at any rate, not only because of that. The Church is catholic, not only because it is an all-embracing entity, not only because it unites all its members, all local Churches, but because it is catholic all through, in its very smallest part, in every act and event of its life. The *nature* of the Church is catholic; the very web of the Church's body is catholic. The Church is catholic, because it is the one Body of Christ; it is union in Christ, oneness in the Holy Ghost—and this unity is the highest wholeness and fulness. The gauge of catholic union is that "the multitude of them that believed be of one heart and of one soul."[21] Where this is not the case, the life of the Church is limited and restricted. The ontological blending of persons is, and must be, accomplished in oneness with the Body of Christ; they cease to be exclusive and impenetrable. The cold separation into "mine" and "thine" disappears.

The growth of the Church is in the perfecting of its inner

wholeness, its inner catholicity, in the "perfection of wholeness"; "that they may be made perfect in one."[22]

The Transfiguration of Personality

The catholicity of the Church has two sides. *Objectively*,
the catholicity of the Church denotes a unity of the Spirit.
"In one Spirit were we all baptized into one body."[23] And
the Holy Spirit which is a Spirit of love and peace, not only
unites isolated individuals, but also becomes in every separate
soul the source of inner peace and wholeness. *Subjectively*,
the catholicity of the Church means that the Church is a
certain unity of life, a brotherhood or communion, a union
of love, "a life in common." The image of the Body is the
commandment of love. "St. Paul demands such love of us,
a love which should bind us one to the other, *so that we no
more should be separated one from the other;* . . . St. Paul
demands that our union should be as perfect as is that of the
members of one body."[24] The novelty of the Christian commandment of love consists in the fact that we are to love our
neighbour as *ourselves*. This is more than putting him on the
same level with ourselves, of identifying him with ourselves;
it means seeing our own self in another, in the beloved one,
not in our own self. . . . Therein lies the limit of love; the
beloved is our "alter ego," an "ego" which is dearer to us
than ourself. In love we are merged into one. "The quality
of love is such that the loving and the beloved are no more
two but one man."[25] Even more: true Christian love sees in
every one of our brethren "Christ Himself." Such love
demands self-surrender, self-mastery. Such love is possible
only in a catholic expansion and transfiguration of the soul.
⊁ The commandment to be catholic is given to every Christian.
The measure of his spiritual manhood is the measure of his
catholicity. The Church is catholic in every one of its members, because a catholic whole cannot be built up or composed
otherwise than through the catholicity of its members. No
multitude, every member of which is isolated and impenetrable, can become a brotherhood. Union can become possible
only through the mutual brotherly love of all the separate

brethren. This thought is expressed very vividly in the well known vision of the Church as of a tower that is being built. (Compare the *Shepherd of Hermas.*) This tower is being built out of separate stones—the faithful. These faithful are "living stones."[26] In the process of building they fit one into the other, because they are smooth and are well adapted to one another; they join so closely to one another, that their edges are no longer visible, and the tower appears to be built of one stone. This is a symbol of unity and wholeness. But notice, only smooth square stones could be used for this building. There were other stones, bright stones, but round ones, and they were of no use for the building; they did not fit one into the other, were not suitable for the building-μὴ ἁρμό- ζοντες-and they had to be placed near the walls.[27] In ancient symbolism "roundness" was a sign of isolation, of self-sufficiency and self-satisfaction—*teres atque rotundus.* And it is just this spirit of self-satisfaction which hinders our entering the Church. The stone must first be made smooth, so that it can fit into the Church wall. We must "reject ourselves" to be able to enter the catholicity of the Church. We must master our self-love in a catholic spirit before we can enter the Church. And in the fulness of the communion of the Church the *catholic transfiguration of personality is accomplished.*

But the rejection and denial of our own self does not signify that personality must be extinguished, that it must be dissolved within the multitude. Catholicity is not corporality or collectivism. On the contrary, *self-denial widens the scope of our own personality; in self-denial we possess the multitude within our own self; we enclose the many within our own ego. Therein lies the similarity with the Divine Oneness of the Holy Trinity.* In its catholicity the Church becomes the created similitude of Divine perfection. The Fathers of the Church have spoken of this with great depth. In the East St. Cyril of Alexandria; in the West St. Hilary.[28] In contemporary Russian theology the Metropolitan Antony has said very adequately, "The existence of the Church can be compared to nothing else upon earth, for on earth there is no unity, but only separation. Only in heaven is there anything like it. The Church is a perfect, a new, a peculiar, a unique existence upon earth, a *unicum,* which cannot be closely defined by any conception taken from the life of the world. The Church is the likeness of the existence of the Holy Trinity, a likeness in which many become one. Why is it that this existence, just as the existence of the Holy Trinity, is new for the old man and unfathomable for him? Because personality in its carnal consciousness is a self-imprisoned existence, radically contrasted with every other personality."[29] "Thus the Christian must *in the measure of his spiritual development* set himself free, making a direct contrast between the 'ego' and the 'non-ego' he must *radically modify the fundamental qualities of human self-consciousness."*[30] It is just in this change that the catholic regeneration of the mind consists.

There are two types of self-consciousness and self-assertion: *separate individualism* and *catholicity.* Catholicity is no denial of personality and catholic consciousness is neither generic nor racial. It is not a common consciousness, neither is it the joint consciousness of the many or the *Bewusstsein ueberhaupt* of German philosophers. Catholicity is achieved not by eliminating the living personality, nor by passing over into the plane of an abstract Logos. *Catholicity is a concrete oneness in thought and feeling.* Catholicity is the style or the order or the setting of *personal* consciousness, which rises to the "level of catholicity." It is the "telos" of personal consciousness, which is realized in creative development, not in the annihilation of personality.

In catholic transfiguration personality receives strength and power to express the life and consciousness of the whole. And this not as an impersonal medium, but in creative and heroic action. We must not say: "Every one in the Church *attains* the level of catholicity," but *"every one can, and must, and is called to attain it."* Not always and not by every one is it attained. In the Church we call those who have attained it Doctors and Fathers, because from them we hear not only their personal profession, but also the testimony of the Church; they speak to us from its catholic completeness, from the completeness of a life full of grace.

The Sacred and The Historical

The Church is the unity of charismatic life. The source of this unity is hidden in the sacrament of the Lord's Supper, and in the sacrament of Pentecost, that unique descent of the Spirit of Truth into the world. Therefore the Church is an *apostolic Church*. It was created and sealed by the Spirit in the Twelve Apostles, and the Apostolic Succession is a living and mysterious thread binding the whole historical fulness of Church life into one catholic whole. Here again we see two sides. The objective side is the uninterrupted sacramental succession, the continuity of the hierarchy. The Holy Ghost does not descend upon earth again and again, but abides in the "visible" and historical Church. And it is in the Church that He breathes and sends forth His rays. Therein lies the fulness and catholicity of Pentecost.

The subjective side is loyalty to the Apostolic tradition; a life spent according to this tradition, as in a living realm of truth. This is the fundamental demand or postulate of Orthodox thought, and here again this demand entails the denial of individualistic separatism; it insists on catholicity. The catholic nature of the Church is seen most vividly in the fact that the experience of the Church belongs to all times. In the life and existence of the Church time is mysteriously overcome and mastered, time, so to speak, *stands still*. It stands still not only because of the power of historical memory, or of imagination, which can "fly over the double barrier of time and space"; it stands still, because of the power of grace, which gathers together in catholic unity of life that which had become separated by walls built in the course of time. Unity in the Spirit embraces in a mysterious, time-conquering fashion, the faithful of all generations. This time-conquering unity is manifested and revealed in the experience of the Church, especially in its Eucharistic experience. The Church is the living image of eternity within time. The experience and life of the Church are not interrupted or broken up by time. This, too, is not only because of continuity in the super-personal outpouring of grace, but also because of the catholic inclusion of all that was, into the mysterious fulness of the present. Therefore the history of the Church gives us not only successive changes, but also identity. In this sense communion with the saints is a *communio sanctorum*. The Church knows that it is a unity of all times, and as such it builds up its life. Therefore the Church thinks of the past not as of something that is no more, but as of something that has been accomplished, as something existing in the catholic fulness of the one Body of Christ. Tradition reflects this victory over time. To learn from tradition, or, still better, *in tradition,* is to learn from the fulness of this time-conquering experience of the Church, an experience which every member of the Church may learn to know and possess according to the measure of his spiritual manhood; according to the measure of his catholic development. It means that we can learn from history as we can from revelation. Loyalty to tradition does not mean loyalty to bygone times and to outward authority; it is a living connexion with the fulness of Church experience. Reference to tradition is no historical inquiry. Tradition is not limited to Church archaeology. Tradition is no outward testimony which can be accepted by an outsider. The Church alone is the living witness of tradition; and only from inside, from within the Church, can tradition be felt and accepted as a certainty. Tradition is the witness of the Spirit; the Spirit's unceasing revelation and preaching of good tidings. For the living members of the Church it is no outward historical authority, but the eternal, continual voice of God—not only the voice of the past, but the voice of eternity. Faith seeks its foundations not merely in the example and bequest of the past, but in the grace of the Holy Ghost, witnessing always, now and ever, world without end.

As Khomyakov admirably puts it, "Neither individuals, nor a multitude of individuals within the Church preserve tradition or write the Scriptures, but the Spirit of God which lives in the whole body of the Church."[31] "Concord with the past" is only the consequence of loyalty to the whole; it is simply the expression of the constancy of catholic experience in the midst of shifting times. To accept and understand tradition we must live within the Church, we must be conscious of the grace-giving presence of the Lord in it; we must feel the breath of the Holy Ghost in it. We may truly say that when we accept tradition we accept, through faith, our Lord, who abides in the midst of the faithful; for the Church is His Body, which cannot be separated from Him. That is why loyalty to tradition means not only *concord* with the past, but, in a certain sense, *freedom from the past,* as from some outward formal criterion. Tradition is not only a protective, conservative principle; it is, primarily, the principle of growth and regeneration. Tradition is not a principle striving to restore the past, using the past as a criterion for the present. Such a conception of tradition is rejected by history itself and by the consciousness of the Church. Tradition is *authority to teach, potestas magisterii, authority to bear witness to the truth.* The Church bears witness to the truth not by reminiscence or from the words of others, but from its own living, unceasing experience, from its catholic fulness. . . . Therein consists that "tradition of truth," *traditio veritatis,* about which St. Irenaeus spoke.[32] For him it is connected with the "veritable unction of truth," *charisma veritatis certum,*[33] and the "teaching of the Apostles" was for him not so much an unchangeable example to be repeated or imitated, as an eternally living and inexhaustible source of life and inspiration. Tradition is the constant abiding of the Spirit and not only the memory of words. Tradition is a *charismatic,* not a historical, principle.

It is quite false to limit the "sources of teaching" to Scripture and tradition, and to separate tradition from Scripture as only an oral testimony or teaching of the Apostles. In the first place, both Scripture and tradition were given only within the Church. Only in the Church have they been received in the fulness of their sacred value and meaning. In them is contained the truth of Divine Revelation, a truth which lives in the Church. This experience of the Church has not been exhausted either in Scripture or in tradition; it is only reflected in them. Therefore, only within the Church does Scripture live and become vivified, only within the Church is it revealed as a whole and not broken up into separate texts, commandments, and aphorisms. This means that Scripture has been *given* in tradition, but not in the sense that it can be understood only according to the dictates of tradition, or that it is the written record of historical tradition or oral teaching. Scripture needs to be explained. It is revealed in theology. This is possible only through the medium of the living experience of the Church.

We cannot assert that Scripture is self-sufficient; and this not because it is incomplete, or inexact, or has any defects, but because Scripture in its very essence does not lay claim to self-sufficiency. We can say that Scripture is a God-inspired scheme or image (*eikon*) of truth, but not truth itself. Strange to say, we often limit the freedom of the Church as a whole, for the sake of furthering the freedom of individual Christians. In the name of individual freedom the Catholic, ecumenical freedom of the Church is denied and limited. The liberty of the Church is shackled by an abstract biblical standard for the sake of setting free individual consciousness from the spiritual demands enforced by the experience of the Church. This is a denial of catholicity, a destruction of catholic consciousness; this is the sin of the Reformation. Dean Inge neatly says of the Reformers: "their creed has been described as a return to the Gospel in the spirit of the Koran."[34] If we declare Scripture to be self-sufficient, we only expose it to subjective, arbitrary interpretation, thus cutting it away from its sacred source. Scripture is given to us in tradition. It is the vital, crystallizing centre. The Church, as the Body of Christ, stands mystically first and is fuller than Scripture. This does not limit Scripture, or cast shadows on it. But truth is revealed to us not only historically. Christ appeared and still appears before us not only in the Scriptures; He unchangeably and unceasingly reveals Himself in the Church, in His own Body. In the times of the early Christians the Gospels were not yet written and could not be the sole source of knowledge. The Church acted according to the spirit of the Gospel, and, what is more, the Gospel came to life in the Church, in the Holy Eucharist. In the Christ of the Eucharist Christians learned to know the Christ of the Gospels, and so His image became vivid to them.

This does not mean that we oppose Scripture to experience. On the contrary, it means that we unite them in the same manner in which they were united from the beginning. We must not think that all we have said denies history. On the contrary, history is recognized in all its sacred realism. As contrasted with outward historical testimony, we put forward no subjective religious experience, no solitary mystical consciousness, not the experience of separate believers, but the integral, living experience of the Catholic Church, catholic experience, and Church life. And this experience includes also historical memory; it is full of history. But this memory is not only a reminiscence and a remembrance of some bygone events. Rather it is a vision of what is, and of what has been, accomplished, a vision of the mystical conquest of time, of the catholicity of the whole of time. The Church knows nought of forgetfulness. The grace-giving experience of the Church becomes integral in its catholic fulness.

This experience has not been exhausted either in Scripture, or in oral tradition, or in definitions. *It cannot, it must not be, exhausted.* On the contrary, all words and images must be regenerated in its experience, not in the psychologisms of subjective feeling, but in experience of spiritual life. This experience is the source of the teaching of the Church. However, not everything within the Church dates from Apostolic times. This does not mean that something has been revealed which was "unknown" to the Apostles; nor does it mean that what is of later date is less important and convincing. Everything was given and revealed fully from the beginning. On the day of Pentecost Revelation was completed, and will admit of no further completion till the Day of Judgment and its last fulfilment. Revelation has not been widened, and even knowledge has not increased. The Church knows Christ now no more than it knew Him at the time of the Apostles. But *it testifies of greater things.* In its definitions it always unchangeably describes the same thing, but in the unchanged image ever new features become visible. But it knows the truth not less and not otherwise than it knew it in time of old. The identity of experience is loyalty to tradition. Loyalty to tradition did not prevent the Fathers of the Church from "creating new names" (as St. Gregory Nazianzen says) when it was necessary for the protection of the unchangeable faith. All that was said later on, was said from catholic complete- ness and is of equal value and force with that which was pro- nounced in the beginning. And even now the experience of the Church has not been exhausted, but protected and fixed in dogma. But there is much of which the Church testifies not in a dogmatic, but in a liturgical, manner, in the symbolism of the sacramental ritual, in the imagery of prayers, and in the established yearly round of commemorations and festivals. Liturgical testimony is as valid as dogmatic testimony. The concreteness of symbols is sometimes even more vivid, clear, and expressive than any logical conceptions can be, as witness the image of the Lamb taking upon Himself the sins of the world.

Mistaken and untrue is that theological minimalism, which wants to choose and set apart the "most important, most certain, and most binding" of all the experiences and teachings of the Church. This is a false path, and a false statement of the question. Of course, not everything in the historical institutions of the Church is equally important and venerable; not everything in the empirical actions of the Church has even been sanctioned. There is much that is only historical. However, we have no outward criterion to discrim- inate between the two. The methods of outward historical criticism are inadequate and insufficient. Only from within the Church can we discern the *sacred* from the *historical*. From within we see what is catholic and belongs to all time, and what is only "theological opinion," or even a simple casual historical accident. Most important in the life of the Church is its fulness, its catholic integrity. There is more freedom in this fulness than in the formal definitions of an enforced minimum, in which we lose what is most impor- tant—directness, integrity, catholicity.

One of the Russian Church historians gave a very success- ful definition of the unique character of the Church's experi- ence. The Church gives us not a system but a key; not a plan of God's City, but the means of entering it. Perhaps someone will lose his way because he has no plan. But all that he will see, he will see without a mediator, he will see it directly, it will be real for him; while he who has studied only the plan, risks remaining outside and not really finding anything.[35]

The Inadequacy of the Vincentian Canon

The well known formula of Vincent of Lerins is very inexact, when he describes the catholic nature of Church life in the words, *Quod ubique, quod semper, quod ab omnibus creditum est.* [What has been believed everywhere, always, and by all]. First of all, it is not clear whether this is an empirical criterion or not. If this be so, then the "Vincentian Canon" proves to be inapplicable and quite false. For about what *omnes* is he speaking? Is it a demand for a general, universal questioning of all the faithful, and even of those who only deem themselves such? At any rate, all the weak and poor of faith, all those who doubt and waver, all those who rebel, ought to be excluded. But the Vincentian Canon gives us no criterion, whereby to distinguish and select. Many disputes arise about faith, still more about dogma. How, then, are we to understand *omnes?* Should we not prove ourselves too hasty, if we settled all doubtful points by leaving the decision to "liberty"—*in dubiis libertas*—according to the well known formula wrongly ascribed to St. Augustine. There is actually no need for universal questioning. Very often the measure of truth is the witness of the minority. It may happen that the Catholic Church will find itself but "a little flock." Perhaps there are more of heterodox than of orthodox mind. It may happen that the heretics spread everywhere, *ubique,* and that the Church is relegated to the background of history, that it will retire into the desert. In history this was more than once the case, and quite possibly it may more than once again be so. Strictly speaking, the Vincentian Canon is something of a tautology. The word *omnes* is to be understood as referring to those that are *orthodox.* In that case the criterion loses its significance. *Idem* is defined *per idem.* And of what eternity and of what omnipresence does this rule speak? To what do *semper* and *ubique* relate? Is it the *experience* of faith or the *definitions* of faith that they refer to? In the latter case the canon becomes a dangerous minimising formula. For not one of the dogmatic definitions strictly satisfies the demand of *semper* and *ubique*.

Will it then be necessary to limit ourselves to the dead letter of Apostolic writings? It appears that the Vincentian Canon is a postulate of historical simplification, of a harmful primitivism. This means that we are not to seek for outward, formal criteria of catholicity; we are not to dissect catholicity in empirical universality. Charismatic tradition is truly universal; in its fulness it embraces every kind of *semper* and *ubique* and unites *all*. But empirically it may not be accepted by all. At any rate we are not to prove the truth of Christianity by means of "universal consent," *per consensum omnium*. In general, no *consensus* can prove truth. This would be a case of acute psychologism, and in theology there is even less place for it than in philosophy. On the contrary, truth is the measure by which we can evaluate the worth of "general opinion." Catholic experience can be expressed even by the few, even by single confessors of faith; and this is quite sufficient. Strictly speaking, to be able to recognize and express catholic truth we need no ecumenical, universal assembly and vote; we even need no "Ecumenical Council." The sacred dignity of the Council lies not in the number of members representing their Churches. A large "general" council may prove itself to be a "council of robbers" (*latrocinium*), or even of apostates. And the *ecclesia sparsa* often convicts it of its nullity by silent opposition. *Numerus episcoporum* does not solve the question. The historical and practical methods of recognizing sacred and catholic tradition can be many; that of assembling Ecumenical Councils is but one of them, and not the only one. This does not mean that it is unnecessary to convoke councils and conferences. But it may so happen that during the council the truth will be expressed by the minority. And what is still more important, the truth may be revealed even without a council. The opinions of the Fathers and of the ecumenical Doctors of the Church frequently have greater spiritual value and finality than the definitions of certain councils. And these opinions do not need to be verified and accepted by "universal consent." On the contrary, it is they themselves who are the criterion and they who can prove. It is of this that the Church testifies in silent *receptio*. Decisive value resides in inner catholicity, not in empirical universality. The opinions of the Fathers are accepted, not as a formal subjection to outward authority, but because of the inner evidence of their catholic truth. The whole body of the Church has the right of verifying, or, to be more exact, the right, and not only the right but the duty, of *certifying*. It was in this sense that in the well known Encyclical Letter of 1848 the Eastern Patriarchs wrote that "the people itself" (λαός), *i.e.* the Body of the Church, "was the guardian of piety" (ὑπερασπιστῆς τῆς Θρησκείας). And even before this the Metropolitan Philaret said the same thing in his Catechism. In answer to the question. "Does a true treasury of sacred tradition exist?" he says *"All the faithful, united through the sacred tradition of faith, all together and all successively, are built up by God into one Church, which is the true treasury of sacred tradition, or, to quote the words of St. Paul, 'The Church of the living God, the pillar and ground of the truth.' "*[36]

The conviction of the Orthodox Church that the "guardian" of tradition and piety is *the whole people, i.e.* the Body of Christ, in no wise lessens or limits the power of teaching given to the hierarchy. It only means that the power of teaching given to the hierarchy is one of the functions of the catholic completeness of the Church; it is the power of testifying, of expressing and speaking the faith and the experience of the Church, which have been preserved in the whole body. The teaching of the hierarchy is, as it were, the mouthpiece of the Church. *De omnium fidelium ore pendeamus, quia in omnem fidelem Spiritus Dei Spirat.* [We depend upon the word of all the faithful, because the Spirit of God breathes in each of the faithful].[37] Only to the hierarchy has it been given to teach "with authority." The hierarchs have received this power to teach, not from the church-people but from the High Priest, Jesus Christ, in the Sacrament of Orders. But this teaching finds its limits in the expression of the whole Church. The Church is called to witness to this experience, which is an inexhaustible experience, a spiritual vision. A bishop of the Church, *episcopus in ecclesia,* must be a teacher. Only the bishop has received full power and authority to speak in the name of his flock. The latter receives the right of speaking through the bishop. But to do so the bishop must embrace his Church within himself; he must make manifest its experience and its faith. He must speak not from himself, but in the name of the Church, *ex consensu ecclesiae.* This is just the contrary of the Vatican formula: *ex sese, non autem ex consensu ecclesiae.* [From himself, but not from the consensus of the Church].

It is not from his flock that the bishop receives full power to teach, but from Christ through the Apostolic Succession. But full power has been given to him to bear witness to the catholic experience of the body of the Church. He is limited by this experience, and therefore in questions of faith the people must judge concerning his teaching. The duty of obedience ceases when the bishop deviates from the catholic norm, and the people have the right to accuse and even to depose him.[38]

Freedom and Authority

In the catholicity of the Church the painful duality and tension between freedom and authority is solved. In the Church there is not and cannot be any outward authority. Authority cannot be a source of spiritual life. So also Christian authority appeals to freedom; this authority must convince, not constrain. Official subjection would in no wise further true unity of mind and of heart. But this does not mean that everyone has received unlimited freedom of personal opinion. It is precisely in the Church that "personal opinions" should not and cannot exist. A double problem is facing every member of the Church. First of all, he must master his subjectivity, set himself free from psychological limitations, raise the standard of his consciousness to its full catholic measure. Secondly, he must live in spiritual sympathy with, and understand, the historical completeness of the Church's experience. Christ reveals Himself not to separate individuals, nor is it only their personal fate which He directs.

Christ came not to the scattered sheep, but to the whole human race, and His work is being fulfilled in the fulness of history, that is, in the Church.

In a certain sense the whole of history is sacred history. Yet, at the same time, the history of the Church is tragic. Catholicity has been given to the Church; its achievement is the Church's task. Truth is conceived in labour and striving. It is not easy to overcome subjectivity and particularism. The fundamental condition of Christian heroism is humility before God, acceptance of His Revelation. And God has revealed Himself in the Church. This is the final Revelation, which passeth not away. Christ reveals Himself to us not in our isolation, but in our mutual catholicity, in our union. He reveals Himself as the New Adam, as the Head of the Church, the Head of the Body. Therefore, humbly and trustfully we must enter the life of the Church and try to find ourselves in it. We must believe that it is just in the Church that the fulness of Christ is accomplished. Every one of us has to face his own difficulties and doubts. But we believe and hope that in united, catholic, heroic effort and exploits, these difficulties will be solved. Every work of fellowship and of concord is a path towards the realization of the catholic fulness of the Church. And this is pleasing in the sight of the Lord:

"Where two or three are gathered together in My name, there am I in the midst of them."[39]

CHAPTER IV

The Church: Her Nature and Task

The Catholic Mind

IT is impossible to start with a formal definition of the
Church. For, strictly speaking, there is none which could
claim any doctrinal authority. None can be found in the
Fathers. No definition has been given by the Ecumenical
Councils. In the doctrinal summaries, drafted on various
occasions in the Eastern Orthodox Church in the seventeenth
century and taken often (but wrongly) for the "symbolic
books," again no definition of the Church was given, except
a reference to the relevant clause of the Creed, followed
by some comments. This lack of formal definitions does not
mean, however, a confusion of ideas or any obscurity of
view. The Fathers did not care so much for the *doctrine* of
the Church precisely because the glorious *reality* of the
Church was open to their spiritual vision. One does not
define what is self-evident. This accounts for the absence of
a special chapter on the Church in all early presentations of
Christian doctrine: in Origen, in St. Gregory of Nyssa, even
in St. John of Damascus. Many modern scholars, both Orthodox and Roman, suggest that the Church itself has not yet
defined her essence and nature. "Die Kirche selbst hat sich
bis heute noch nicht definiert," says Robert Grosche.[1] Some
theologians go even further and claim that no definition of

"The Church: Her Nature and Task" appeared in volume I of the
Universal Church in God's Design (S.C.M. Press, 1948).

the Church is possible.[2] In any case, the theology of the Church is still *im Werden,* in the process of formation.[3]

In our time, it seems, one has to get beyond the modern theological disputes, to regain a wider historical perspective, to recover the true "catholic mind," which would embrace the whole of the historical experience of the Church in its pilgrimage through the ages. One has to return from the school-room to the worshipping Church and perhaps to change the school-dialect of theology for the pictorial and metaphorical language of Scripture. The very nature of the Church can be rather depicted and described than properly defined. And surely this can be done only from within the Church. Probably even this description will be convincing only for those of the Church. The Mystery is apprehended only by faith.

The New Reality

The Greek name *ekklesia* adopted by the primitive Christians to denote the New Reality, in which they were aware they shared, presumed and suggested a very definite conception of what the Church really was. Adopted under an obvious influence of the Septuagint use, this word stressed first of all the organic continuity of the two Covenants. The Christian existence was conceived in the sacred perspective of the Messianic preparation and fulfilment (Heb. i, 1-2). A very definite theology of history was thereby implied. The Church was the true Israel, the new Chosen People of God, "a chosen generation, a holy nation, a peculiar people" (1 Pet. ii, 9). Or rather, it was the faithful Remnant, selected out of the unresponsive People of old.[4] And all nations of the earth, Greeks and Barbarians, were to be coopted and grafted into this new People of God by the call of God (this was the main theme of St. Paul in Romans and Galatians—cf. Ephesians ch. ii).

Already in the Old Testament the word *ekklesia* (a rendering in Greek of the Hebrew *Qahal*) did imply a special emphasis on the ultimate unity of the Chosen People, conceived as a sacred whole, and this unity was rooted more in the mystery of the divine election than in any "natural" features. This emphasis could only be confirmed by the supplementary influence of the Hellenistic use of the word *ekklesia* meaning usually an assembly of the sovereign people in a city, a general congregation of all regular citizens. Applied to the new Christian existence, the word kept its traditional connotation. The Church was both the People and the City. A special stress has been put on the organic unity of Christians.

Christianity from the very beginning existed as a corporate reality, as a community. To be Christian meant just to belong to the community. Nobody could be Christian by himself, as an isolated individual, but only together with "the brethren," in a "togetherness" with them. *Unus Christianus—nullus Christianus.* [One Christian—no Christian]. Personal conviction or even a rule of life still do not make one a Christian. Christian existence presumes and implies an incorporation, a membership in the community. This must be qualified at once: in the *Apostolic* community, i.e. in communion with the Twelve and their message. The Christian "community" was gathered and constituted by Jesus Himself "in the days of His flesh," and it was given by Him at least a provisional constitution by the election and the appointment of the Twelve, to whom He gave the name (or rather the title) of His "messengers" or "ambassadors."[5] For a "sending forth" of the Twelve was not only a mission, but precisely a commission, for which they were invested with a "power" (Mark iii, 15; Matt. x, 1; Luke ix, 1). In any case as the appointed "witnesses" of the Lord (Luke xxiv, 48; Acts i, 8) the Twelve alone were entitled to secure the continuity both of the Christian message and of the community life. Therefore communion with the Apostles was a basic note of the primitive "Church of God" in Jerusalem (Acts ii, 42: *koinonia*).

Christianity means a "common life," a life in common. Christians have to regard themselves as "brethren" (in fact this was one of their first names), as members of one corporation, closely linked together. And therefore charity had to be the first mark and the first proof as well as the token of this fellowship. We are entitled to say: Christianity *is* a community, a corporation, a fellowship, a brotherhood, a "society," *coetus fidelium*. And surely, as a first approximation, such a description could be of help. But obviously it requires a further qualification, and something crucial is missing here. One has to ask: in what exactly this unity and togetherness of the many is based and rooted? what is the power that brings many together and joins them one with another? Is this merely a social instinct, some power of social cohesion, an impetus of mutual affection, or any other natural attraction? Is this unity based simply on unanimity, on identity of views or convictions? Briefly, is the Christian Community, the Church, merely a human society, a society of men? Surely, the clear evidence of the New Testament takes us far beyond this purely human level. Christians are united not only among themselves, but first of all they *are* *one—in Christ,* and only this communion *with* Christ makes the communion of men first possible—*in* Him. The centre of unity *is the Lord* and the power that effects and enacts the unity *is the Spirit.* Christians are constituted into this unity by divine design; by the Will and Power of God. Their unity comes from above. They are one only in Christ, as those who had been born anew in Him, "rooted and built up in Him" (Col. ii, 7), who by One Spirit have been "baptized into One Body" (1 Cor. xii, 13). The Church of God has been established and constituted by God through Jesus Christ, Our Lord: "she is His own creation by water and the word." Thus there is no human society, but rather a "Divine Society," not a secular community, which would have been still "of this world," still commensurable with other human groups, but a sacred community, which is intrinsically "not of this world," not even of "this aeon," but of the "aeon to come."

Moreover, Christ Himself belongs to this community, as its Head, not only as its Lord or Master. Christ is not above or outside of the Church. The Church *is in Him.* The Church is not merely a community of those who believe in Christ and walk in His steps or in His commandments. She is a community of those who abide and dwell in Him, and in whom He Himself is abiding and dwelling by the Spirit. Christians

are set apart, "born anew" and re-created, they are given not
only a new pattern of life, but rather a new principle: the new
Life in the Lord by the Spirit. They are a "peculiar People,"
"the People of God's own possession." The point is that the
Christian Community, the *ekklesia,* is a *sacramental community*: *communio in sacris,* a "fellowship in holy things,"
i.e. in the Holy Spirit, or even *communio sanctorum* (*sanctorum* being taken as neuter rather than masculine—perhaps
that was the original meaning of the phrase). The unity of
the Church is effected through the sacraments: Baptism and
the Eucharist are the two "social sacraments" of the Church,
and in them the true meaning of Christian "togetherness" is
continually revealed and sealed. Or even more emphatically,
the sacraments constitute the Church. Only in the sacraments
does the Christian Community pass beyond the purely human
measure and become the Church. Therefore "the right administration of the sacraments" belongs to the essence of the
Church (to her *esse*). Sacraments must be "worthily" received
indeed, therefore they cannot be separated or divorced from
the inner effort and spiritual attitude of believers. Baptism
is to be preceded by repentance and faith. A personal relation
between an aspirant and his Lord must be first established by
the hearing and the receiving of the Word, of the message of
salvation. And again an oath of allegiance to God and His
Christ is a pre-requisite and indispensable condition of the
administration of the sacrament (the first meaning of the
word *sacramentum* was precisely "the [military] oath.") A
catechumen is already "enrolled" among the brethren on
the basis of his faith. Again, the baptismal gift is appro-
priated, received and kept, by faith and faithfulness, by the
steadfast standing in the faith and the promises. And yet
sacraments are not merely signs of a professed faith, but
rather effective signs of the saving Grace—not only symbols
of human aspiration and loyalty, but the outward symbols of
the divine action. In them our human existence is linked to,
or rather raised up to, the Divine Life, by the Spirit, the
giver of life.

　　The Church as a whole is a *sacred* (or consecrated) community, distinguished thereby from "the (profane) world."

She is the *Holy Church*. St. Paul obviously uses the terms "Church" and "saints" as co-extensive and synonymous. It is remarkable that in the New Testament the name "saint" is almost exclusively used in the plural, saintliness being social in its intrinsic meaning. For the name refers not to any human achievement, but to a gift, to sanctification or consecration. Holiness comes from the Holy One, i.e. only from God. To be holy for a man means to share the Divine Life. Holiness is available to individuals only in the community, or rather in the "fellowship of the Holy Spirit." The "communion of saints" is a pleonasm. One can be a "saint" only in the communion.

Strictly speaking, the Messianic Community, gathered by Jesus the Christ, was not yet the Church, before His Passion and Resurrection, before "the promise of the Father" was sent upon it and it was "endued with the power from on high," "baptized with the Holy Spirit" (cf. Luke xxiv, 49 and Acts i, 4-5), in the mystery of Pentecost. Before the victory of the Cross disclosed in the glorious Resurrection, it was still *sub umbraculo legis*. [Under the Shadow of the law]. It was still the eve of the fulfilment. And Pentecost was there to witness to and to seal the victory of Christ. "The power from on high" has entered into history. The "new aeon" has been truly disclosed and started. And the sacramental life of the Church is the continuation of Pentecost.

The descent of the Spirit was a supreme revelation. Once and for ever, in the "dreadful and inscrutable mystery" of Pentecost, the Spirit-Comforter enters the world in which He was not yet present in such manner as now He begins to dwell and to abide. An abundant spring of living water is disclosed on that doy, here on earth, in the world which had been already redeemed and reconciled with God by the Crucified and Risen Lord. The Kingdom comes, for the Holy Spirit is the Kingdom.[6] But the "coming" of the Spirit depends upon the "going" of the Son (John xvi, 7). "Another Comforter" comes down to testify of the Son, to reveal His glory and to seal His victory (xv, 26; xvi, 7 and 14). Indeed in the Holy Spirit the Glorified Lord

Himself comes back or returns to His flock to abide with them always (xiv, 18 and 28).... Pentecost was the mystical consecration, the baptism of the whole Church (Acts i, 5). This fiery baptism was administered by the Lord: for He baptizes "with the Holy Spirit and with fire" (Matt. iii, 111 and Luke iii, 16). He has sent the Spirit from the Father, as a pledge in our hearts. The Holy Spirit is the spirit of adoption, in Christ Jesus, "the power of Christ" (2 Cor. xii, 9). By the spirit we recognize and we acknowledge that Jesus is the Lord (1 Cor. xii 3). The work of the Spirit in believers is precisely their incorporation into Christ, their baptism into one body (xii, 13), even the body of Christ. As St. Athanasius puts it: "being given drink of the Spirit, we drink Christ." For the Rock was Christ.[7]

By the Spirit Christians are united with Christ, are united in Him, are constituted into His Body. *One body,* that of Christ: this excellent analogy used by St. Paul in various contexts, when depicting the mystery of Christian existence, is at the same time the best witness to the intimate experience of the Apostolic Church. By no means was it an accidental image: it was rather a summary of faith and experience. With St. Paul the main emphasis was always on the intimate union of the faithful with the Lord, on their sharing in His fulness. As St. John Chrysostom has pointed out, commenting on Col. iii, 4, in all his writings St. Paul was endeavouring to prove that the believers "are in communion with Him in all things" and "precisely to show this union does he speak of the Head and the body."[8] It is highly probable that the term was suggested by the Eucharistic experience (cf. 1 Cor. x, 17), and was deliberately used to suggest its sacramental connotation. The Church of Christ is one in the Eucharist, for the Eucharist is Christ Himself, and He *sacramentally* abides in the Church, which is His Body. The Church is a body indeed, *an organism,* much more than a society or a corporation. And perhaps an "organism" is the best modern rendering of the term *to soma,* as used by St. Paul.

Still more, the Church is the *body of Christ* and His "fulness" *Body* and *fulness* (*to soma* and *to pleroma*)—

these two terms are correlative and closely linked together in St. Paul's mind, one explaining the other: "which is His body, the fulness of Him Who all in all is being fulfilled" (Eph. i, 23). The Church is the Body of Christ because it is His *complement*. St. John Chrysostom commends the Pauline idea just in this sense. "The Church is the complement of Christ in the same manner in which the head completes the body and the body is completed by the head." Christ is not alone. "He has prepared the whole race in common to follow Him, to cling to Him, to accompany His train." Chrysostom insists, "Observe how he (i.e. St. Paul) introduces Him as having need of all the members. This means that only then will the Head be filled up, when the Body is rendered perfect, when we are all together, co-united and knit together."[9] In other words, the Church is the extension and the "fulness" of the Holy Incarnation, or rather of the Incarnate life of the Son, "with all that for our sakes was brought to pass, the Cross and tomb, the Resurrection the third day, the Ascension into Heaven, the sitting on the right hand" (Liturgy of St. John Chrysostom, Prayer of Consecration).

The Incarnation is being completed in the Church. And, in a certain sense, the Church is Christ Himself, in His all-embracing plenitude (cf. 1 Cor. xii, 12). This identification has been suggested and vindicated by St. Augustine: *"Non solum nos Christianos factos esse, sed Christum."* [Not only to make us Christians, but Christ.] For if He is the Head, we are the members: the whole man is He and we—*"totus homo, ille et nos—Christus et Ecclesia."* And again: "For Christ is not simply in the head and not in the body (only), but Christ is entire in the head and body"—*"non enim Christus in capite et non in corpore, sed Christus totus in capite et in corpore."*[10] This term *totus Christus*[11] occurs in St. Augustine again and again, this is his basic and favourite idea, suggested obviously by St. Paul. "When I speak of Christians in the plural, I understand one in the One Christ. Ye are therefore many, and ye are yet one: we are many and we are one"—*"cum plures Christianos appello, in uno Christo unum intelligo."*[12] "For our

Lord Jesus is not only in Himself, but in us also"—
"*Dominus enim Jesus non solum in se, sed et in nobis.*"[13]
"One Man up to the end of the ages"—"*Unus homo usque
ad finem saeculi extenditur.*"[14]

The main contention of all these utterances is obvious.
Christians are incorporated into Christ and Christ abides in
them—this intimate union constitutes the mystery of the
Church. The Church is, as it were, the place and the mode
of the redeeming presence of the Risen Lord in the redeemed world. "The Body of Christ is Christ Himself. The
Church is Christ, as after His Resurrection He is present
with us and encounters us here on earth."[15] And in this
sense one can say: Christ is the Church. "*Ipse enim est
Ecclesia, per sacramentum corporis sui in se ... eam con-
tinens.*"[16] [For He himself is the Church, containing it in
himself through the sacrament of his body.] Or in the
words of Karl Adam: "Christ, the Lord, is the proper Ego
of the Church."[17]

The Church is the unity of charismatic life. The source
of this unity is hidden in the sacrament of the Lord's
Supper and in the mystery of Pentecost. And Pentecost is
continued and made permanent in the Church by means
of the Apostolic Succession. It is not merely, as it were, the
canonic skeleton of the Church. Ministry (or "hierarchy")
itself is primarily a *charismatic* principle, a "ministry of
the sacraments," or "a divine oeconomia." Ministry is not
only a *canonical* commission, it belongs not only to the
institutional fabric of the Church—it is rather an indispensable constitutional or *structural* feature, just in so far as
the Church is a body, an organism. Ministers are not, as it
were, "commissioned officers" of the community, not only
leaders or delegates of the "multitudes," of the "people" or
"congregation"—they are acting not only *in persona ecclesiae.*
They are acting primarily *in persona Christi.* They are "rep-
resentatives" of Christ Himself, not of believers, and in
them and through them, the Head of the Body, the only
High Priest of the New Covenant, is performing, continuing and accomplishing His eternal pastoral and priestly
office. He is Himself the only true Minister of the Church.

All others are but stewards of His mysteries. They are standing *for* Him, *before* the community—and just because the Body is one only in its Head, is brought together and into unity by Him and in Him, the Ministry in the Church is primarily the Ministry of unity. In the Ministry the organic unity of the Body is not only represented or exhibited, but rather rooted, without any prejudice to the "equality" of the believers, just as the "equality" of the cells of an organism is not destroyed by their structural differentiation: all cells are equal as such, and yet differentiated by their functions, and again this differentiation serves the unity, enables this organic unity to become more comprehensive and more intimate. The unity of every local congregation springs from the unity in the Eucharistic meal. And it is as the celebrant of the Eucharist that the priest is the minister and the builder of Church unity. But there is another and higher office: to secure the universal and catholic unity of the whole Church in space and time. This is the episcopal office and function. On the one hand, the Bishop has an authority to ordain, and again this is not only a jurisdictional privilege, but precisely a power of sacramental action beyond that possessed by the piest. Thus the Bishop as "ordainer" is the builder of Church unity on a wider scale. The Last Supper and Pentecost are inseparably linked to one another. The Spirit Comforter descends when the Son has been glorified in His death and resurrection. But still they are two sacraments (or mysteries) which cannot be merged into one another. In the same way the priesthood and the episcopate differ from one another. In the episcopacy Pentecost becomes universal and continuous, in the undivided episcopate of the Church (*episcopatus unus* of St. Cyprian) the unity in space is secured. On the other hand, through its bishop, or rather in its bishop, every particular or local Church is included in the catholic fulness of the Church, is linked with the past and with all ages. In its bishop every single Church outgrows and transcends its own limits and is organically united with the others. The Apostolic Succession is not so much the canonical as the mystical foundation of Church unity. It is something other than a safeguard of historical continuity or of administrative cohesion. It is an ultimate means to keep the mystical identity of the Body through the ages. But, of course, Ministry is never detached from the Body. It is in the Body, belongs to its structure. And ministerial gifts are given inside the Church (cf. 1 Cor. xii).

The Pauline conception of the Body of Christ was taken up and variously commented on by the Fathers, both in the East and in the West, and then was rather forgotten.[18] It is high time now to return to this experience of the early Church which may provide us with a solid ground for a modern theological synthesis. Some other similes and metaphors were used by St. Paul and elsewhere in the New Testament, but much to the same purpose and effect: *to stress the intimate and organic unity between Christ and those who are His.* But, among all these various images, that of the Body is the most inclusive and impressive, is the most emphatic expression of the basic vision.[19] Of course, no analogy is to be pressed too far or over-emphasized. The idea of an organism, when used of the Church, has its own limitations. On the one hand, the Church is composed of human personalities, which never can be regarded merely as elements or cells of the whole, because each is in direct and immediate union with Christ and His Father—the personal is not to be sacrificed or dissolved in the corporate, Christian "togetherness" must not degenerate into impersonalism. The idea of the organism must be supplemented by the idea of a symphony of personalities, in which the mystery of the Holy Trinity is reflected (cf. John xvii, 21 and 23), and this is the core of the conception of "catholicity" (sobornost).[20] This is the chief reason why we should prefer a christological orientation in the theology of the Church rather than a pneumatological.[21] For, on the other hand, the Church, as a whole, has her *personal centre* only in Christ, she is not an incarnation of the Holy Spirit, nor is she merely a Spirit-being community, but precisely the Body of Christ, the Incarnate Lord. This saves us from impersonalism without committing us to any humanistic personification. Christ the Lord is the only Head and the only Master of the Church. "In Him the whole structure is closely fitted together and grows into a temple holy in the Lord; in Him you too are being built together into a dwelling-place for God in the Spirit (Eph. ii, 21-22, Bp. Challoner's version).

The Christology of the Church does not lead us into the misty clouds of vain speculations or dreamy mysticism. On the contrary, it secures the only solid and positive ground for proper theological research. The doctrine of the Church finds thereby its proper and organic place in the general scheme of the Divine Oeconomia of salvation. For we have indeed still to search for a comprehensive vision of the mystery of our salvation, of the salvation of the world.

One last distinction is to be made. The Church is still *in statu viae* and yet it is already *in statu patriae*. It has, as it were, a double life, *both in heaven and on earth.*[22] The Church is a visible historical society, and the same is the Body of Christ. It is both the Church of the redeemed, and the Church of the miserable sinners—both at once. On the historical level no *final* goal has yet been attained. But the *ultimate* reality has been disclosed and revealed. This ultimate reality is still at hand, is truly available, in spite of the historical imperfection, though but in provisional forms. For the Church is a sacramental society. *Sacramental* means no less than *"eschatological." To eschaton* does not mean primarily *final,* in the temporal series of events; it means rather *ultimate* (decisive); and the ultimate is being realized within the stress of historical happenings and events. What is "not of this world" is here "in this world," not abolishing this world, but giving to it a new meaning and a new value, "transvaluating" the world, as it were. Surely this is still only an anticipation, a "token" of the final consummation. Yet the Spirit abides in the Church. This constitutes the mystery of the Church: a visible "society" of frail men *is* an organism of the Divine Grace.[23]

The New Creation

The primary task of the historical Church is the proc-

lamation of another word "to come." The Church bears
witness to the New Life, disclosed and revealed in Christ
Jesus, the Lord and Saviour. This it does both by word and
deed. The true proclamation of the Gospel would be
precisely the practice of this New Life: to show faith by
deeds (cf. Matt. v, 16).

The Church is more than a company of preachers, or a
teaching society, or a missionary board. It has not only to
invite people, but also to introduce them into this New
Life, to which it bears witness. It is a missionary body indeed, and its missionfield is the whole world. But the aim
of its missionary activity is not merely to convey to people
certain convictions or ideas, not even to impose on them a
definite discipline or a rule of life, but first of all to introduce them into the New Reality, to *convert* them, to
bring them through their faith and repentance to Christ
Himself, that they should be born anew in Him and into
Him by water and the Spirit. Thus the ministry of the
Word is completed in the ministry of the Sacraments.

"Conversion" is a fresh start, but it is only a start, to
be followed by a long process of growth. The Church has
to organize the new life of the converted. The Church has,
as it were, to exhibit the new pattern of existence, the new
mode of life, that of the "world to come." The Church
is here, in this world, for its salvation. But just for this
reason it has to oppose and to renounce *"this"* word. God
claims the whole man, and the Church bears witness to this
"totalitarian" claim of God revealed in Christ. The Christian has to be a "new creation." Therefore he cannot find
a settled place for himself within the limits of the "old
world." In this sense the Christian attitude is, as it were,
always revolutionary with regard to the "old order" of
"this world." Being "not of this world" the Church of
Christ "in this world" can only be in permanent opposition, even if it claims only a reformation of the existing
order. In any case, the change is to be radical and total.

Historical Antinomies

Historical failures of the Church do not obscure the absolute and ultimate character of its challenge, to which it is committed by its very eschatological nature, and it constantly challenges itself.

Historical life and the task of the Church are an antinomy, and this antinomy can never be solved or overcome on a historical level. It is rather a permanent hint to what is "to come" hereafter. The antinomy is rooted in the practical alternative which the Church had to face from the very beginning of its historical pilgrimage. *Either* the Church was to be constituted as an exclusive and "totalitarian" society, endeavouring to satisfy all requirements of the believers, both "temporal" and "spiritual," paying no attention to the existing order and leaving nothing to the external world—it would have been an entire separation from the world, an ultimate flight out of it, and a radical denial of any external authority. *Or* the Church could attempt an inclusive Christianization of the world, subduing the whole of life to Christian rule and authority, to reform and to reorganize secular life on Christian principles, to build the Christian City. In the history of the Church we can trace both solutions: a flight to the desert and a construction of the Christian Empire. The first was practiced not only in monasticism of various trends, but in many other Christian groups and denominations. The second was the main line taken by Christians, both in the West and in the East, up to the rise of militant secularism, but even in our days this solution has not lost its hold on many people. But on the whole, both proved unsuccessful. One has, however, to acknowledge the reality of their common problem and the truth of their common purpose. Christianity is not an individualistic religion and it is not only concerned for the "salvation of the soul." Christianity is the Church, i.e. a Community, the New People of God, leading its corporate life according to its peculiar principles. And this life cannot be split into departments, some of which might have been ruled by any other and heterogeneous principles. Spiritual leadership of the Church can hardly be reduced to an occasional guidance given to individuals or to groups living under conditions utterly uncongenial to the Church. The legitimacy of these conditions must be questioned first of all. The task of a complete re-creation or re-shaping of the whole fabric of human life cannot or must not be avoided or declined. One cannot serve two Masters and a double allegiance is a poor solution. Here the above-mentioned alternative inevitably comes in—everything else would merely be an open compromise or a reduction of the ultimate and therefore *total* claims. *Either* Christians ought to go out of the world, in which there is another Master besides Christ (whatever name this other Master may bear: Caesar or Mammon or any other) and in which the rule and the goal of life are other than those set out in the Gospel—to go out and to start a separate society. *Or* again Christians have to transform the outer world, to make it the Kingdom of God as well, and introduce the principles of the Gospel into secular legislation.

There is an inner consistency in both programmes. And therefore the separation of the two ways is inevitable. Christians seem compelled to take different ways. The unity of the Christian task is broken. An inner schism arises within the Church: an abnormal separation between the monks (or the *elite* of the initiated) and the lay-people (including clergy), which is far more dangerous than the alleged "clericalization" of the Church. In the last resort, however, it is only a symptom of the ultimate antinomy. The problem simply has no historical solution. A true solution would transcend history, it belongs to the "age to come." In this age, on the historic plane, no constitutional principle can be given, but only a regulative one: a principle of discrimination, not a principle of construction.

For again each of the two programmes is self-contradictory. There is an inherent *sectarian* temptation in the first: the "catholic" and universal character of the Christian message and purpose is here at least obscured and often deliberately denied, the world is simply left out of sight. And all attempts at the direct Christianization of the world, in the guise of a Christian State or Empire, have only led to the more or less acute *secularization* of Christianity itself.[24]

In our time nobody would consider it possible for everyone to be converted to a universal monasticism or a realization of a truly Christian, and universal, State. The Church remains "in the world," as a heterogeneous body, and the tension is stronger than it has ever been; the ambiguity of the situation is painfully felt by everyone in the Church. A practical programme for the present age can be deduced only from a restored understanding of the nature and essence of the Church. And the failure of all Utopian expectations cannot obscure the Christian hope: the King has come, the Lord Jesus, and His Kingdom is to come.

CHAPTER V

The Function of Tradition
In the Ancient Church

"Ego vero Evangelio non crederem, ni si me catholicae Ecclesiae commoveret auctoritas." [Indeed, I should not have believed the Gospel, if the authority of the Catholic Church had not moved me].

ST. AUGUSTINE, contra epist. Manichaei, I.1.

St. Vincent of Lérins and Tradition

THE FAMOUS *dictum* of St. Vincent of Lérins was characteristic of the attitude of the Ancient Church in the matters of faith: *teneamus quod ubique, quod semper, quod ab omnibus creditum est.* ["We must hold what has been believed everywhere, always, and by all." *Commonitorium,* 2.] This was at once the criterion and the norm. The crucial emphasis was here on the permanence of Christian teaching. St. Vincent was actually appealing to the double "ecumenicity" of Christian faith—in space and in time. In fact, it was the same great vision which had inspired St. Irenaeus in his own time: the One Church, expanded and scattered in the whole world, and yet speaking with one voice, holding the same faith everywhere, as it had been handed down by the blessed Apostles and preserved by the succession of witnesses:

"The Function of Tradition in the Ancient Church" appeared in *The Greek Orthodox Theological Review* (IX, 2, 1963). Copyright by *The Greek Orthodox Theological Review* and reprinted with permission.

*quae est ab apostolis, quae per successionem presbyterorum
in ecclesiis custoditur.* ["Which is being preserved in the
Church from the Apostles through the succession of the
presbyters."] These two aspects of faith, or rather—the two
dimensions, could never be separated from each other. *Universitas* and *antiquitas,* as well as *consensio,* belonged together. Neither was an adequate criterion by itself. "Antiquity"
as such was not yet a sufficient warrant of truth, unless a
comprehensive *consensus* of the "ancients" could be satis-
factorily demonstrated. And *consensio* as such was not con-
clusive, unless it could be traced back continuously to Apostolic origins. Now, suggested St. Vincent, the true faith could
be recognized by a double recourse—to Scripture and Tradition: *duplici modo ... primum scilicet divinae legis auctori-
tate, tum deinde ecclesiae catholicae traditione.* ["In two
ways ... first clearly by the authority of the Holy Scriptures,
then by the tradition of the Catholic Church."] This did not
imply, however, that there were two sources of Christian
doctrine. Indeed, the rule, or canon, of Scripture was "perfect" and "self-sufficient"—*ad omnia satis superque sufficiat.*
["For all things complete and more than sufficient."] Why
then should it be supplemented by any other "authority"?
Why was it imperative to invoke also the authority of "ecclesiastical understanding"—*ecclesiasticae intelligentiae auctoritas?* The reason was obvious: Scriptures were differently
interpreted by individuals: *ut paene quot homines tot illinc
sententiae erui posse videantur.* ["So that one might almost
gain the impression that it can yield as many different meanings, as there are men."] To this variety of "private" opinions
St. Vincent opposes the "common" mind of the Church, the
mind of the Church Catholic: *ut propheticae et apostolicae
interpretationis linea secundum ecclesiastici et catholici sensus
normam dirigatur.* ["That the trend of the interpretation of
the prophets and the apostolic writings be directed in accordance with the rule of the ecclesiastical and Catholic
meaning."] Tradition was not, according to St. Vincent, an
independent instance, nor was it a complementary source of
faith. "Ecclesiastical understanding" could not add anything
to the Scripture. But it was the only means to ascertain and

to disclose the true meaning of Scripture. Tradition was, in fact, the authentic interpretation of Scripture. And in this sense it was co-extensive with Scripture. Tradition was actually "Scripture rightly understood." And Scripture was for St. Vincent the only, primary and ultimate, *canon* of Christian truth (*Commonitorium,* cap. II, cf. cap. XXVIII).

The Hermeneutical Question in the Ancient Church

At this point St. Vincent was in full agreement with the established tradition. In the admirable phrase of St. Hilary of Poitiers, *scripturae enim non in legendo sunt, sed in intelligendo.* ["For Scripture is not in the reading, but in the understanding"; *ad Constantium Aug.,* lib. II, cap. 9, ML X, 570; the phrase is repeated also by St. Jerome, *Dial. c. Lucifer.,* cap. 28, ML XXIII, 190-191]. The problem of right exegesis was still a burning issue in the Fourth century, in the contest of the Church with the Arians, no less than it has been in the Second century, in the struggle against Gnostics, Sabellians, and Montanists. All parties in the dispute used to appeal to Scripture. Heretics, even Gnostics and Manichees, used to quote Scriptural texts and passages and to invoke the authority of the Holy Writ. Moreover, exegesis was at that time the main, and probably the only, theological method, and the authority of the Scripture was sovereign and supreme. The Orthodox were bound to raise the crucial hermeneutical question: What was the principle of interpretation? Now, in the Second century the term "Scriptures" denoted primarily the Old Testament and, on the other hand, the authority of these "Scriptures" was sharply challenged, and actually repudiated, by the teaching of Marcion. The Unity of the Bible had to be proved and vindicated. What was the basis, and the warrant, of Christian, and Christological, understanding of "Prophesy," that is—of the Old Testament? It was in this historical situation that the authority of Tradition was first invoked. Scripture belonged to the Church, and it was only in the Church, within the community of right faith, that Scripture could be adequately understood and correctly interpreted. Heretics, that is—those outside of the

Church, had no key to the mind of the Scripture. It was not enough just to read and to quote Scriptural words—the true meaning, or intent, of Scripture, taken as an integrated whole, had to be elicited. One had to grasp, as it were—in advance, the true pattern of Biblical revelation, the great design of God's redemptive Providence, and this could be done only by an insight of faith. It was by faith that *Christuszeugniss* could be discerned in the Old Testament. It was by faith that the unity of the tetramorph Gospel could be properly ascertained. But this faith was not an arbitrary and subjective insight of individuals—it was the faith of the Church, rooted in the Apostolic message, or *kerygma,* and authenticated by it. Those outside of the Church were missing precisely this basic and overarching message, the very heart of the Gospel. With them Scripture was just a dead letter, or an array of disconnected passages and stories, which they endeavored to arrange or re-arrange on their own pattern, derived from alien sources. They had another faith. This was the main argument of Tertullian in his passionate treatise *De praescriptione.* He would not discuss Scriptures with heretics—they had no right to use Scriptures, as they did not belong to them. Scriptures were the Church's possession. Emphatically did Tertullian insist on the priority of the "rule of faith," *regula fidei.* It was the only key to the meaning of the Scripture. And this "rule" was Apostolic, was rooted in, and derived from, the Apostolic preaching. C. H. Turner has rightly described the meaning and the intention of this appeal or reference to the "rule of faith" in the Early Church. "When Christians spoke of the 'Rule of Faith' as 'Apostolic,' they did not mean that the Apostles had met and formulated it. . . . What they meant was that the profession of belief which every catechumen recited before his baptism did embody in summary form the faith which the Apostles had taught and had committed to their disciples to teach after them." This profession was the same everywhere, although the actual phrasing could vary from place to place. It was always intimately related to the baptismal formula.[1] Apart from this "rule" Scripture could be but misinterpreted. Scripture and Tradition were indivisibly interwined for Tertullian.

*Ubi enim apparuerit esse veritatem disciplinae et fidei chris-
tianae, illic erit veritas scripturarum et expositionum et
omnium traditionum christianarum.* ["For only where the
true Christian teaching and faith are evident will the true
Scriptures, the true interpretations, and all the true Christian
traditions be found"; XIX. 3]. The Apostolic Tradition of
faith was the indispensable guide in the understanding of
Scripture and the ultimate warrant of right interpretation.
The Church was not an external authority, which had to
judge over the Scripture, but rather the keeper and guardian
of that Divine truth which was stored and deposited in the
Holy Writ.[2]

St. Irenaeus and the "Canon of Truth"

Denouncing the Gnostic mishandling of Scriptures, St.
Irenaeus introduced a picturesque simile. A skillful artist has
made a beautiful image of a king, composed of many precious
jewels. Now, another man takes this mosaic image to pieces,
re-arranges the stones on another pattern so as to produce
the image of a dog or of a fox. Then he starts claiming that
this was the original picture, by the first master, under the
pretext that the gems (the ψηφίδες) were authentic. In fact,
however, the original design had been destroyed—λύσας
τὴν ὑποκειμένην τοῦ ἀνθρώπου ἰδέαν. This is precisely
what the heretics do with the Scripture. They disregard and
disrupt "the order and connection" of the Holy Writ and
"dismember the truth"—λύοντες τὰ μέλη τῆς ἀληθείας.
Words, expressions, and images—ῥήματα, λέξεις, παρα-
βολαὶ—are genuine, indeed, but the design, the ὑπόθεσις,
is arbitrary and false (*adv. hoeres.,* 1. 8. 1). St. Irenaeus suggested as well another analogy. There were in circulation at
that time certain *Homerocentones,* composed of genuine
verses of Homer, but taken at random and out of context,
and re-arranged in arbitrary manner. All particular verses
were truly Homeric, but the new story, fabricated by the
means of re-arrangement, was not Homeric at all. Yet, one
could be easily deceived by the familiar sound of the Homeric
idiom (1. 9. 4). It is worth noticing that Tertullian also

refers to these curious *centones,* made of Homeric or Virgilian verses (*de praescr.,* XXXIX). Apparently, it was a common device in the polemical literature of that time. Now, the point which St. Irenaeus endeavored to make is obvious. Scripture had its own pattern or design, its internal structure and harmony. The heretics ignore this pattern, or rather substitute their own instead. In other words, they re-arrange the Scriptural evidence on a pattern which is quite alien to the Scripture itself. Now, contended St. Irenaeus, those who had kept unbending that "canon of truth" which they had received at baptism, will have no difficulty in "restoring each expression to its appropriate place" (τῇ ἰδίᾳ τάξει). Then they are able to behold the true image. The actual phrase used by St. Irenaeus is peculiar: προσαρμόσας τῷ τῆς ἀληθείας σωμάτιῳ (which is clumsily rendered in the old Latin translation as *corpusculum veritatis*). But the meaning of the phrase is quite clear. The σωμάτιον is not necessarily a diminutive. It simply denotes a "corporate body." In the phrase of St. Irenaeus it denotes the *corpus* of truth, the right context, the original design, the "true image," the original disposition of gems and verses.[3] Thus, for St. Irenaeus, the reading of Scripture must be guided by the "rule" of faith—to which believers are committed (and into which they are initiated) by their baptismal profession, and by which only the basic message, or "the truth," of the Scripture can be adequately assessed and identified. The favorite phrase of St. Irenaeus was "the rule of truth," κανὼν τῆς ἀληθείας, *regula veritatis.* Now, this "rule" was, in fact, nothing else than the witness and preaching of the Apostles, their κήρυγμα and *praedicatio* (or *praeconium*), which was "deposited" in the Church and entrusted to her by the Apostles, and then was faithfully kept and handed down, with complete unanimity in all places, by the succession of accredited pastors: *qui cum episcopatus successione charisma veritatis certum acceperunt.* [Those who, together with the succession of the episcopacy, have received the firm charisma of truth; IV. 26. 2]. Whatever the direct and exact connotation of this pregnant phrase may be,[4] there can be no doubt that, in the mind of St. Irenaeus, this continuous pres-

ervation and transmission of the deposited faith was operated
and guided by the abiding presence of the Holy Spirit in the
Church. The whole conception of the Church in St. Irenaeus
was at once "charismatic" and "institutional." And "Tradition" was, in his understanding, a *depositum juvenescens,*
[a living tradition] entrusted to the Church as a new breath
of life, just as breath was bestowed upon the first man—(*que-
madmodum aspiratio plasmationis* III. 24. 1). Bishops or
"presbyters" were in the Church accredited guardians and
ministers of this once deposited truth. "Where, therefore, the
charismata of the Lord have been deposited (*posita sunt*),
there is it proper to learn the truth, namely from those who
have that succession of the Church which is from the Apostles
(apud quos est ea quae est ab apostolis ecclesiae successio),
and who display a sound and blameless conduct and an
unadulterated and incorrupt speech. For these also preserve
this faith of ours in one God who created all things, and
they increase that love for the Son of God, who accomplished
such marvellous dispensation for our sake, and they expound
the Scriptures to us without danger, neither blaspheming God,
nor dishonoring the patriarchs, nor despising the prophets"
(IV. 26. 5).

The Regula Fidei

Tradition was in the Early Church, first of all, an hermeneutical principle and method. Scripture could be rightly
and fully assessed and understood only in the light and in the
context of the living Apostolic Tradition, which was an
integral factor of Christian existence. It was so, of course, not
because Tradition could add anything to what has been
manifested in the Scripture, but because it provided that living
context, the comprehensive perspective, in which only the
true "intention" and the total "design" of the Holy Writ,
of Divine Revelation itself, could be detected and grasped.
The truth was, according to St. Irenaeus, a "well-grounded
system," a *corpus* (*adv. haeres.* II. 27. 1—*veritatis corpus*), a
"harmonious melody" (II. 38. 3). But it was precisely this
"harmony" which could be grasped only by the insight of

faith. Indeed, Tradition was not just a transmission of inherited doctrines, in a "Judaic manner," but rather the continuous life in the truth.[5] It was not a fixed core or complex
of binding propositions, but rather an insight into the meaning and impact of the revelatory events, of the revelation of
the "God who acts." And this was determinative in the field
of Biblical exegesis. G. L. Prestige has well put it: "The
voice of the Bible could be plainly heard only if its text were
interpreted broadly and rationally, in accordance with the
apostolic creed and the evidence of the historical practice of
Christendom. It was the heretics that relied on isolated texts,
and the Catholics who paid more attention on the whole to
scriptural principles."[6] Summarizing her careful analysis of
the use of Tradition in the Early Church, Dr. Ellen Flesseman-
van-Leer has written: "Scripture without interpretation is not
Scripture at all; the moment it is used and becomes alive it
is always interpreted Scripture." Now, Scripture must be
interpreted "according to its own basic purport," which is
disclosed in the *regula fidei.* Thus, this *regula* becomes, as it
were, the controlling instance in the exegesis. "Real interpretation of Scripture is Church preaching, is tradition."[7]

St. Athanasius and the "Scope of Faith"

The situation did not change in the Fourth century. The
dispute with the Arians was centered again in the exegetical
field,—at least, in its early phase. The Arians and their sup-
porters have produced an impressive array of Scriptural texts
in the defense of their doctrinal position. They wanted to
restrict theological discussion to the Biblical ground alone.
Their claims had to be met precisely on this ground, first of
all. And their exegetical method, the manner in which they
handled the text, was much the same as that of the earlier
dissenters. They were operating with selected proof-texts,
without much concern for the total context of the Revelation.
It was imperative for the Orthodox to appeal to the mind of
the Church, to that "Faith" which had been once delivered
and then faithfully kept. This was the main concern, and the
usual method, of St. Athanasius. The Arians quoted various

passages from the Scripture to substantiate their contention that the Saviour was a creature. In reply St. Athanasius invoked the "rule of faith." This was his usual argument. "Let us, who possess τὸν σκοπὸν τῆς πίστεως [the scope of faith], restore the correct meaning (ὀρθὴν τὴν διάνοιαν) of what they had wrongly interpreted" (*c. Arian.* III. 35). St. Athanasius contended that the "correct" interpretation of particular texts was only possible in the total perspective of faith. "What they now allege from the Gospels they explain in an unsound sense, as we may discover if we take in consideration τὸν σκοπὸν τῆς καθ᾽ ἡμᾶς τοὺς Χριστιανοὺς πίστεως [the scope of the faith according to us Christians], and read the Scripture using it (τὸν σκοπὸν) as the rule—ὥσπερ κανόνι χρησάμενοι." (III. 28) On the other hand, close attention must be given also to the immediate context and setting of every particular phrase and expression, and the exact intention of the writer must be carefully identified (I. 54). Writing to Bishop Serapion, on the Holy Spirit, St. Athanasius contends again that Arians ignored or missed "the scope of the Divine Scripture"— μὴ εἰδόντες τὸν σκοπὸν τῆς Θείας Γραφῆς (*ad Serap.,* II. 7; cf. *ad episc. Eg.,* 4: τὰ λεγόμενα μόνον σκοπῶν, καὶ μὴ τὴν διάνοιαν θεωρῶν). The σκοπὸς was, in the language of St. Athanasius, a close equivalent of what St. Irenaeus used to denote as ὑπόθεσις,—the underlying "idea," the true design, the intended meaning.[8] On the other hand, the word σκοπὸς was a habitual term in the exegetical language of certain philosophical schools, especially in Neoplatonism. Exegesis played a great role in the philosophical endeavor of that time, and the question of hermeneutical principle had to be raised. Jamblichos was, for one, quite formal at this point. One had to discover the "main point," or the basic theme, of the whole treatise under examination, and to keep it all time in mind.[9] St. Athanasius could well be acquainted with the technical use of the term. It was misleading, he contended, to quote isolated texts and passages, disregarding the total intent of the Holy Writ. It is obviously inaccurate to interpret the term σκοπὸς in the idiom of St. Athanasius as "the general drift" of the Scripture. The "scope" of the faith, or of the Scripture, is precisely their credal core, which is condensed in the "rule of faith," as it had been maintained in the Church and "transmitted from fathers to fathers," while the Arians had "no fathers" for their opinions (*de decr.*, 27). As Cardinal Newman has rightly observed, St. Athanasius regarded the "rule of faith" as an ultimate "principle of interpretation," opposing the "ecclesiastical sense" (τὴν ἐκκλησιαστικὴν διάνοιαν, *c. Arian.* I. 44) to "private opinions" of the heretics.[10] Time and again, in his scrutiny of the Arian arguments, St. Athanasius would summarize the basic tenets of the Christian faith, before going into the actual re-examination of the alleged proof-texts, in order to restore texts into their proper perspective. H. E. W. Turner has described this exegetical manner of St. Athanasius:

> Against the favorite Arian technique of pressing the grammatical meaning of a text without regard either to the immediate context or to the wider frame of reference in the teaching of the Bible as a whole, he urges the need to take the general drift of the Church's Faith as a Canon of interpretation. The Arians are blind to the wide sweep of Biblical theology and therefore fail to take into sufficient account the context in which their proof-texts are set. The sense of Scripture must itself be taken as Scripture. This has been taken as a virtul abandonment of the appeal to Scripture and its replacement by an argument from Tradition. Certainly in less careful hands it might lead to the imposition of a strait-jacket upon the Bible as the dogmatism of Arian and Gnostic had attempted to do. But this was certainly not the intention of St. Athanasius himself. For him it represents an appeal from exegesis drunk to exegesis sober, from a myopic insistence upon the grammatical letter to the meaning of intention (σκοπός, χαρακτήρ) of the Bible.[11]

It seems, however, that Professor Turner exaggerated the danger. The argument was still strictly scriptural, and, in principle, St. Athanasius admitted the sufficiency of the Scripture, sacred and inspired, for the defense of truth (*c. Gentes,* I). Only Scripture had to be interpreted in the context of the living credal tradition, under the guidance or control of the "rule of faith." This "rule," however, was in no sense an "extraneous" authority which could be "imposed" on the Holy Writ. It was the same "Apostolic preaching," which was written down in the books of the New Testament, but it was, as it were, this preaching *in epitome*. St. Athanasius writes to Bishop Serapion: "Let us look at that very tradition, teaching, and faith of the Catholic Church from the very beginning, which the Lord gave (ἔδωκεν), the Apostles preached (ἐκήρυξαν), and the Fathers preserved (ἐφύλαξαν). Upon this the Church is founded" (*ad Serap.*, I. 28). The passage is highly characteristic of St. Athanasius. The three terms in the phrase actually coincide: παράδοσις [tradition]—from Christ himself, διδασκαλία [teaching]—by the Apostles, and πίστις [faith]—of the Catholic Church. And this is the foundation (θεμέλιον) of the Church—a sole and single foundation.[12] Scripture itself seems to be subsumed and included in this "Tradition," coming, as it is, from the Lord. In the concluding chapter of his first epistle to Serapion St. Athanasius returns once more to the same point. "In accordance with the Apostolic faith delivered to us by tradition from the Fathers, I have delivered the tradition, without inventing anything extraneous to it. What I learned, that have I inscribed (ἐνεχάραξα), conformably with the Holy Scriptures" (c. 33). On an occasion St. Athanasius denoted the Scripture itself as an Apostolic *paradosis* (*ad Adelph.*, 6). It is characteristic that in the whole discussion with the Arians no single reference was made to any "traditions"—in plural. The only term of reference was always "Tradition,"—indeed, *the* Tradition, the Apostolic Tradition, comprising the total and integral content of the Apostolic "preaching," and summarized in the "rule of faith." The unity and solidarity of this Tradition was the main and crucial point in the whole argument.

The Purpose of Exegesis and the "Rule of Worship"

The appeal to Tradition was actually an appeal to the mind of the Church. It was assumed that the Church had the knowledge and the understanding of the truth, of the truth and the "meaning" of the Revelation. Accordingly, the Church had both the competence and the authority to proclaim the Gospel and to interpret it. This did not imply that the Church was "above" the Scripture. She stood by the

Scripture, but on the other hand, was not bound by its "letter." The ultimate purpose of exegesis and interpretation was to elicit the meaning and the intent of the Holy Writ, or rather the meaning of the Revelation, of the *Heils-geschichte.* The Church had to preach Christ, and not just "the Scripture." The use of Tradition in the Ancient Church can be adequately understood only in the context of the actual use of the Scripture. The Word was kept alive in the Church. It was reflected in her life and structure. Faith and Life were organically interwined. It would be proper to recall at this point the famous passage from the *Indiculus de gratia Dei,* which was mistakenly attributed to Pope Celestine and was in fact composed by St. Prosper of Aquitania: "These are the inviolable decrees of the Holy and Apostolic See by which our holy Fathers slew the baneful innovation...Let us regard the sacred prayers which, in accordance with apostolic tradition our priests offer uniformly in every Catholic Church in all the world. Let the rule of worship lay down the rule of faith." It is true, of course, that this phrase in its immediate context was not a formulation of a general principle, and its direct intention was limited to one particular point: Infant Baptism as an instance pointing to the reality of an inherited or original sin. Indeed, it was not an authoritative proclamation of a Pope, but a private opinion of an individual theologian, expressed in the context of a heated controversy.[13] Yet, it was not just an accident, and not a misunderstanding, that the phrase had been taken out of its immediate context and slightly changed in order to express the principle: *ut legem credendi statuat lex orandi.* [So that the rule of worship should establish the rule of faith]. "Faith" found its first expression precisely in the liturgical,—sacramental, rites and formulas—and "Creeds" first emerged as an integral part of the rite of initiation. "Credal summaries of faith, whether interrogatory or declaratory, were a by-product of the liturgy and reflected its fixity or plasticity," says J. N. D. Kelly.[13] "Liturgy," in the wide and comprehensive sense of the word, was the first and initial layer in the Tradition of the Church, and the argument from the *lex orandi* [Rule of worship] was persistently used in discussion already by the end of the Second century. The Worship of the Church was a solemn proclamation of her Faith. The baptismal invocation of the Name was probably the earliest Trinitarian formula, as the Eucharist was the primary witness to the mystery of Redemption, in all its fulness. The New Testament itself came to existence, as a "Scripture," in the Worshipping Church. And Scripture was read first in the context of worship and meditation.

St. Basil and "Unwritten Tradition"

Already St. Irenaeus used to refer to "faith" as it had been received at baptism. Liturgical arguments were used by Tertullian and St. Cyprian.[14] St. Athanasius and the Cappadocians used the same argument. The full development of this argument from the liturgical tradition we find in St. Basil. In his contest with the later Arians, concerning the Holy Spirit, St. Basil built his major argument on the analysis of doxologies, as they were used in the Churches. The treatise of St. Basil, *De Spiritu Sancto,* was an occasional tract, written in the fire and heat of a desperate struggle, and addressed to a particular historic situation. But St. Basil was concerned here with the principles and methods of theological investigation. In his treatise St. Basil was arguing a particular point,—indeed, the crucial point in the sound Trinitarian doctrine,—the *homotimia* of the Holy Ghost. His main reference was to a liturgical witness: the doxology of a definite type (*"with the Spirit"*), which, as he could demonstrate, has been widely used in the Churches. The phrase, of course, was not in the Scripture. It was only attested by tradition. But his opponents would not admit any authority but that of the Scripture. It is in this situation that St. Basil endeavored to prove the legitimacy of an appeal to Tradition. He wanted to show that the ὁμοτιμία of the Spirit, that is, his Divinity, was always believed in the Church and was a part of the Baptismal profession of faith. Indeed, as Père Benoit Pruche has rightly observed, the ὁμότιμος was for St. Basil an equivalent of the ὁμοούσιος.[15] There was little new in this concept of Tradition, except consistency and precision.

His phrasing, however, was rather peculiar. "Of the dog-mata and kerygmata, which are kept in the Church, we have some from the written teaching (ἐκ τῆς ἐγγράφου διδα-σκαλίας), and some we derive from the Apostolic *paradosis,* which had been handed down ἐν μυστηρίῳ. And both have the same strength—τὴν αὐτὴν ἰσχύν—in the matters of piety" (*de Spir. S.,* 66). At first glance one may get the impression that St. Basil introduces here a double authority and double standard—Scripture *and* Tradition. In fact he was very far from doing so. His use of terms is peculiar. *Kerygmata* were for him what in the later idiom was usually denoted as "dogmas" or "doctrines"—a formal and authoritative teaching and ruling in the matters of faith,—the open or public teaching. On the other hand, *dogmata* were for him the total complex of "unwritten habits" (τὰ ἄγραφα τῶν ἐθνῶν), or, in fact, the whole structure of liturgical and sacramental life. It must be kept in mind that the concept, and the term itself, "dogma," was not yet fixed by that time,—it was not yet a term with a strict and exact connotation.[16] In any case, one should not be embar-rassed by the contention of St. Basil that *dogmata* were delivered or handed down, by the Apostles, ἐν μυστηρίῳ. It would be a flagrant mistranslation if we render it as "in secret." The only accurate rendering is: "by the way of mysteries," that is—under the form of rites and (litur-gical) usages, or "habits." In fact, it is precisely what St. Basil says himself: τὰ πλεῖστα τῶν μυστικῶν ἀγρά-φως ἡμῖν ἐμπολιτεύεται. [Most of the mysteries are communicated to us by an unwritten way]. The term τὰ μυστικά refers here, obviously, to the rites of Baptism and Eucharist, which are, for St. Basil, of "Apostolic" origin. He quotes at this point St. Paul's own reference to "tradi-tions," which the faithful have received (εἴτε διὰ λόγου, εἴτε δι' ἐπιστολῆς II Thess. 2:15; I Cor. 11:2). The doxology in question is one of these "traditions" (71; cf. also 66—οἱ τὰ περὶ τὰς Ἐκκλησίας ἐξαρχῆς δια-θεσμοθετήσαντες ἀπόστολοι καὶ πατέρες, ἐν τῷ κεκρυμμένῳ καὶ ἀφθέγκτῳ τὸ σεμνὸν τοῖς μυστη-ρίοις ἐφύλασσον). [The Apostles and Fathers who from the very beginning arranged everything in the churches, preserved the sacred character of the mysteries in silence and secrecy]. Indeed, all instances quoted by St. Basil in this connection are of ritual or liturgical nature: the use of the sign of the Cross in the rite of admission of Catechumens; the orientation toward East at prayer; the habit to keep standing at worship on Sundays; the *epiclesis* in the Eucharistic rite; the blessing of water and oil, the renunciation of Satan and his pomp, the triple immersion, in the rite of Baptism. There are many other "unwritten mysteries of the Church," says St. Basil: τὰ ἄγραφα τῆς ἐκκλησίας μυστήρια (c. 66 and 67). They are not mentioned in the Scripture. But they are of great authority and significance. They are indispensable for the preservation of right faith. They are effective means of witness and communication. According to St. Basil, they come from a "silent" and "private" tradition: ἀπὸ τῆς σιωπωμένης καὶ μυστικῆς παραδόσεως· ἐκ τῆς ἀδημοσιεύτου ταύτης καὶ ἀπορρήτου διδασκαλίας. [From the silent and mystical tradition, from the unpublic and ineffable teaching]. This "silent" and "mystical" tradition, "which has not been made public," is not an esoteric doctrine, reserved for some particular elite. The "elite" was the Church. In fact, "tradition" to which St. Basil appeals, is the liturgical practice of the Church. St. Basil is referring here to what is now denoted as *disciplina arcani*. [The discipline of secrecy]. In the fourth century this "discipline" was in wide use, was formally imposed and advocated in the Church. It was related to the institution of the Catechumenate and had primarily an educational and didactic purpose. On the other hand, as St. Basil says himself, certain "traditions" had to be kept "unwritten" in order to prevent profanation at the hands of the infidel. This remark obviously refers to rites and usages. It may be recalled at this point that, in the practice of the Fourth century, the Creed (and also the Dominical Prayer) were a part of this "discipline of secrecy" and could not be disclosed to the non-initiated. The Creed was reserved for the candidates for Baptism, at the last stage of their instruction, after they had been solemnly enrolled and approved. The Creed was communicated, or "traditioned," to them by the bishop *orally* and they had to recite it by memory before him: the ceremony of *traditio* and *redditio symboli*. [Transmission and Repetition (by the initiated) of the Creed]. The Catechumens were strongly urged not to divulge the Creed to outsiders and not to commit it to writing. It had to be inscribed in their hearts. It is enough to quote there the *Procatechesis* of St. Cyril of Jerusalem, cap 12 and 17. In the West Rufinus and St. Augustine felt that it was improper to set the Creed down on paper. For that reason Sozomen in his *History* does not quote the text of the Nicene Creed, "which only the initiated and the mystagogues have the right to recite and hear" (*hist. eccl.* 1.20). It is against this background, and in this historic context, that the argument of St. Basil must be assessed and interpreted. St. Basil stresses strongly the importance of the Baptismal profession of faith, which included a formal commitment to the belief in the Holy Trinity, Father, Son, and Holy Spirit (67 and 26). It was a "tradition" which had been handed down to the neophytes "in mystery" and had to be kept "in silence." One would be in great danger to shake "the very foundation of the Christian faith"—τὸ στερέωμα τῆς εἰς Χριστὸν πίστεως—if this "unwritten tradition" was set aside, ignored, or neglected (c. 25). The only difference between δόγμα and κήρυγμα was in the manner of their transmission: dogma is kept "in silence" and *kerygmata* are "publicized": τὸ μὲν γὰρ σιωπᾶται, τὰ δὲ κηρύγματα δημοσιεύονται. But their intent is identical: they convey the same faith, if in different manners. Moreover, this particular habit was not just a tradition of the Fathers—such a tradition would not have sufficed: οὐκ ἐξαρκεῖ. In fact, "the Fathers" derived their "principles" from "the intention of the Scripture"—τῷ βουλήματι τῆς Γραφῆς ἠκολούθησαν, ἐκ τῶν μαρτυριῶν . . . τὰς ἀρχὰς λαβόντες. [Following the intention of the Scripture, deriving their principles from the scriptural witnesses]. Thus, the "unwritten tradition," in rites and symbols, does not actually add anything to the content of the Scriptural faith: it only puts this faith in focus.[17]

St. Basil's appeal to "unwritten tradition" was actually an appeal to the faith of the Church, to her *sensus catholicus,* to the φρόνημα ἐκκλησιαστικόν. [Ecclesiastical mind]. He had to break the deadlock created by the obstinate and narrow-minded *pseudo-biblicism* of his Arian opponents. And he pleaded that, apart from this "unwritten" rule of faith, it was impossible to grasp the true intention and teaching of the Scripture itself. St. Basil was strictly scriptural in his theology: Scripture was for him the supreme criterion of doctrine (*epist.* 189.3). His exegesis was sober and reserved. Yet, Scripture itself was a mystery, a mystery of Divine "economy" and of human salvation. There was an inscrutable depth in the Scripture, since it was an "inspired" book, a book by the Spirit. For that reason the true exegesis must be also spiritual and prophetic. A gift of spiritual discernment was necessary for the right understanding of the Holy Word. "For the judge of the words ought to start with the same preparation as the author ... And I see that in the utterances of the Spirit it is also impossible for everyone to undertake the scrutiny of His word, but only for them who have the Spirit which grants the discernment" (*epist.* 204). The Spirit is granted in the sacraments of the Church. Scripture must be read in the light of faith, and also in the community of the faithful. For that reason Tradition, the tradition of faith as handed down through generations, was for St. Basil an indispensable guide and companion in the study and interpretation of the Holy Writ. At this point he was following in the steps of St. Irenaeus and St. Athanasius. In the similar way Tradition, and especially the liturgical witness, of the Church was used by St. Augustine.[18]

The Church as Interpreter of Scripture

since she was the only authentic depository of Apostolic
The Church had the authority to interpret the Scripture,

kerygma. This *kerygma* was unfailingly kept alive in the Church, as she was endowed with the Spirit. The Church was still teaching *viva voce,* commending and furthering the Word of God. And *viva vox Evangelii* [the living voice of the Gospel] was indeed not just a recitation of the words of the Scripture. It was a proclamation of the Word of God, as it was heard and preserved in the Church, by the ever abiding power of the quickening Spirit. Apart from the Church and her regular Ministry, "in succession" to the Apostles, there was no true proclamation of the Gospel, no sound preaching, no real understanding of the Word of God. And therefore it would be in vain to look for truth elsewhere, outside of the Church, Catholic and Apostolic. This was the common assumption of the Ancient Church, from St. Irenaeus down to Chalcedon, and further. St. Irenaeus was quite formal at this point. In the Church the fullness of truth has been gathered by the Apostles: *plenissime in eam contulerint omnia quae sunt veritatis* [lodged in her hands most copiously are all things pertaining to truth (*adv. hoeres.,* III.4.1)]. Indeed, Scripture itself was the major part of this Apostolic "deposite." So was also the Church. Scripture and Church could not be separated, or opposed to each other. Scripture, that is—its true understanding, was only in the Church, as she was guided by the Spirit. Origen was stressing this unity between Scripture and Church persistently. The task of the interpreter was to disclose the word of the Spirit: *hoc observare debemus ut non nostras, cum docemus, sed Sancti Spiritus sententias proferamus* [we must be careful when we teach to present not our own interpretation but that of the Holy Spirit (*in Rom.,* 1.3.1.)]. And this is simply impossible apart from the Apostolic Tradition, kept in the Church. Origen insisted on *catholic* interpretation of Scripture, as it is offered in the Church: *audiens in Ecclesia verbum Dei catholice tractari* [hearing in the Church the Word of God presented in the catholic manner (*in Lev. hom.,* 4.5)]. Heretics, in their exegesis, ignore precisely the true "intention" or the *voluntas* of the Scripture: *qui enim neque juxta voluntatem Scripturarum neque juxta fidei veritatem profert eloquia Dei, seminat triticum et metit spinas* [those who present the words of God, not in conjunction with the intention of the Scriptures, nor in conjunction with the truth of faith, have sown wheat and reaped thorns (*in Jerem. hom.*, 7.3)]. The "intention" of the Holy Writ and the "Rule of faith" are intimately correlated and correspond to each other. This was the position of the Fathers in the Fourth century and later, in full agreement with the teaching of the Ancients. With his usual sharpness and vehemence of expression, St. Jerome, this great man of Scripture, has voiced the same view:

> Marcion and Basilides and other heretics . . . do not possess the Gospel of God, since they have no Holy Spirit, without which the Gospel so preached becomes human. We do not think that Gospel consists of the words of Scripture but in its meaning; not on the surface but in the marrow, not in the leaves of sermons but in the root of meaning. In this case Scripture is really useful for the hearers when it is not spoken without Christ, nor is presented without the Fathers, and those who are preaching do not introduce it without the Spirit . . . It is a great danger to speak in the Church, lest by a perverse interpretation of the Gospel of Christ, a gospel of man is made . . . (in Galat., I, 1. II; M. L. XXVI, c. 386)

There is the same preoccupation with the true understanding of the Word of God as in the days of St. Irenaeus, Tertullian, and Origen. St. Jerome probably was simply paraphrasing Origen. Outside of the Church there is no "Divine Gospel," but only human substitutes. The true meaning of Scripture, the *sensus Scripturae,* that is—the *Divine message,* can be detected only *juxta fidei veritatem* [in conjunction with the truth of faith], under the guidance of the rule of faith. The *veritas fidei* [the truth of faith] is, in this context, the Trinitarian confession of faith. It is the same approach as in St. Basil. Again, St. Jerome is speaking here primarily of the proclamation of the Word in the Church: *andientibus utilis est* [to those who hear the Word].

St. Augustine and Catholic Authority

In the same sense we have to interpret the well known,

and justly startling, statement of St. Augustine: *Ego vero Evangelio non crederem, nisi me catholicae Ecclesiae commoveret auctoritas* [Indeed, I should not have believed the Gospel, if the authority of the Catholic Church had not moved me (*c. epistolam Fundamenti,* v.6)]. The phrase must be read in its context. First of all, St. Augustine did not utter this sentence on his own behalf. He spoke of the attitude which a simple believer had to take, when confronted with the heretical claim for authority. In this situation it was proper for a simple believer to appeal to the authority of the Church, from which, and in which, he had received the Gospel itself: *ipsi Evangelio catholicis praedicantibus credidi.* [I believed the Gospel itself, being instructed by catholic preachers]. The Gospel and the preaching of the *Catholica* belong together. St. Augustine had no intention "to subordinate" the Gospel to the Church. He only wanted to emphasize that "Gospel" is actually received always in the context of Church's catholic preaching and simply cannot be separated from the Church. Only in this context it can be assessed and properly understood. Indeed, the witness of the Scripture is ultimately "self-evident," but only for the "faithful," for those who have achieved a certain "spiritual" maturity,—and this is only possible within the Church. He opposed this teaching and preaching *auctoritas* of the Church Catholic to the pretentious vagaries of Manichean exegesis. The Gospel did not belong to the Manicheans. *Catholicae Ecclesiae auctoritas* [the authority of the Catholic Church] was not an independent source of faith. But it was the indispensable principle of sound interpretation. Actually, the sentence could be converted: one should not believe the Church, unless one was moved by the Gospel. The relationship is strictly reciprocal.[19]

CHAPTER VI

The Authority of the Ancient Councils
And the Tradition of the Fathers

The Councils in the Early Church

THE SCOPE of this essay is limited and restricted. It is no more than an introduction. Both subjects—the role of the Councils in the history of the Church and the function of Tradition—have been intensively studied in recent years. The purpose of the present essay is to offer some suggestions which may prove helpful in the further scrutiny of documentary evidence and in its theological assessment and interpretation. Indeed, the ultimate problem is ecclesiological. The Church historian is inevitably also a theologian. He is bound to bring in his personal options and commitments. On the other hand, it is imperative that theologians also should be aware of that *wide historical perspective* in which matters of faith and doctrine have been continuously discussed and comprehended. Anachronistic language must be carefully avoided. Each age must be discussed on its own terms.

The student of the Ancient Church must begin with the study of particular Councils, taken in their concrete historical setting, against their specific existential background, without attempting any overarching definition in advance. Indeed, it

"The Authority of the Ancient Councils and the Tradition of the Fathers" appeared in *Glaube, Geist, Geschichte: Festschrift für Ernst Benz zum* 60. *Geburtstag am* 17. *November* 1967 (Leiden: E. J. Brill, 1967). Reprinted with permission from E. J. Brill.

is precisely what historians are doing. There was no "Conciliar theory" in the Ancient Church, no elaborate "theology
of the Councils," and even no fixed canonical regulations.
The Councils of the Early Church, in the first three centuries, were occasional meetings, convened for special pur-
poses, usually in the situation of urgency, to discuss particular
items of common concern. They were *events,* rather than an
institution. Or, to use the phrase of the late Dom Gregory
Dix, "in the pre-Nicene times Councils were an occasional
device, with no certain place in the scheme of Church government."[1] Of course, it was commonly assumed and agreed,
already at that time, that meeting and consultation of bishops,
representing or rather personifying their respective local
churches or "communities," was a proper and normal method
to manifest and to achieve the unity and consent in matters
of faith and discipline. The sense of the Unity of the Church
was strong in Early times, although it had not yet been
reflected on the organizational level. The "collegiality"
of the bishops was assumed in principle and the concept of
the *Episcopatus unus* was already in the process of formation.
Bishops of a particular area used to meet for the election
and consecration of new bishops. Foundations had been laid
for the future Provincial or Metropolitan system. But all
this was rather a spontaneous movement. It seems that
"Councils" came into existence first in Asia Minor, by the
end of the second century, in the period of intensive defense
against the spread of the "New Prophecy," that is, of the
Montanist enthusiastic explosion. In this situation it was but
natural that the main emphasis should be put on "Apostolic
Tradition," of which bishops were guardians and witnesses
in their respective *paroikiai.* It was in North Africa that a
kind of Conciliar system was established in the third century.
It was found that Councils were the best device for witnessing, articulating, and proclaiming the common mind of the
Church and the accord and unanimity of local churches.
Professor Georg Kretschmar has rightly said, in his recent
study on the Councils of the Ancient Church, that the basic
concern of the Early Councils was precisely with the Unity
of the Church: "*Schon von ihrem Ursprung her ist ihr eigent-*

liches Thema aber das Ringen um die rechte, geistliche Einheit der Kirche Gottes.''[2] Yet, this Unity was based on the identity of Tradition and the unanimity in faith, rather than on any institutional pattern.

The Imperial or Ecumenical Council

The situation changed with the Conversion of the Empire. Since Constantine, or rather since Theodosius, it has been commonly assumed and acknowledged that Church was co-extensive with Commonwealth, that is, with the Universal Empire which has been christened. The "Conversion of the Empire" made the Universality of the Church more *visible* than ever before. Of course, it did not add anything to the essential and intrinsic Universality of the Christian Church. But the new opportunity provided for its visible manifestation. It was in this situation that the first General Council was convened, the Great Council of Nicea. It was to become the model for the later Councils. "The new established position of the Church necessitated *ecumenical* action, precisely because Christian life was now lived in the world which was no longer organized on a basis of localism, but of the Empire as a whole . . . Because the Church has come out into the world the local churches had to learn to live no longer as self-contained units (as in practice, though not in theory, they have largely lived in the past), but as parts of a vast spiritual government."[3] In a certain sense the General Councils as inaugurated at Nicea may be described as "Imperial Councils," *die Reichskonzile,* and this was probably the first and original meaning of the term "Ecumenical" as applied to the Councils.[4] It would be out of place now to discuss at any length the vexed and controversial problem of the nature or character of that peculiar structure which was the new Christian Commonwealth, the theocratic *Res publica Christiana,* in which the Church was strangely wedded with the Empire.[5] For our immediate purpose it is actually irrelevant. The Councils of the fourth century were still occasional meetings, or individual *events,* and their ultimate authority was still

grounded in their conformity with the "Apostolic Tradition."
It is significant that no attempt to develop a legal or canonical theory of "General Councils," as a seat of ultimate
authority, with specific competence and models of procedure,
was made at that time, in the fourth century, or later, although they were *de facto* acknowledged as a proper instance
to deal with the questions of faith and doctrine and as an
authority on these matters. It will be no exaggeration to
suggest that Councils were never regarded as a canonical
institution, but rather as occasional *charismatic events*. Councils were not regarded as periodical gatherings which had
to be convened at certain fixed dates. And no Council was
accepted as valid in advance, and many Councils were actually disavowed, in spite of their formal regularity. It is enough
to mention the notorious Robber Council of 449. Indeed,
those Councils which were actually recognized as "Ecumenical," in the sense of their binding and infallible authority,
were recognized, immediately or after a delay, not because
of their formal *canonical* competence, but because of their
charismatic character: under the guidance of the Holy Spirit
they have witnessed to the Truth, in conformity with the
Scripture as handed down in Apostolic Tradition.[6] There is
no space now to discuss *the theory of reception*. In fact, there
was *no theory*. There was simply an *insight* into the matters
of faith. Hans Küng, in his recent book, *Strukturen der
Kirche,* has suggested a helpful avenue of approach to this
very problem. Indeed, Dr. Küng is not a historian, but his
theological scheme can be fruitfully applied by historians.
Kung suggested that we should regard the Church herself
as a "Council," an Assembly, and as a Council convened by
God Himself, *aus göttlicher Berufung,* and the historic Councils, that is, the Ecumenical or General Councils, as Councils
aus menschlicher Berufung, as a "representation" of the
Church,—indeed, a "true representation," but yet no more
than a representation.[7] It is interesting to note that a similar
conception had been made already many years ago by the
great Russian Church historian, V. V. Bolotov, in his *Lectures
on the History of the Ancient Church*. Church is *ecclesia,*
an assembly, which is never adjourned.[8] In other words, the

ultimate authority — and the ability to discern the truth in faith — is vested in the Church which is indeed a "Divine institution," in the proper and strict sense of the word, whereas no Council, and no "Conciliar institution," is *de jure Divino,* except in so far as it happens to be a true image or manifestation of the Church herself. We may seem to be involved here in a vicious circle. We may be actually involved in it, if we insist on *formal* guarantees in doctrinal matters. But, obviously, such "guarantees" do not exist and cannot be produced, especially in advance. Certain "Councils" were actually failures, no more than *conciliabula,* and did err. And for that reason they were subsequently disavowed. The story of the Councils in the fourth century is, in this respect, very instructive.[9] The claims of the Councils were accepted or rejected in the Church not on formal or "canonical" ground. And the verdict of the Church has been highly selective. *The Council is not above the Church,* this was the attitude of the Ancient Church. The Council is precisely a "representation." This explains why the Ancient Church never appealed to "Conciliar authority" in general or *in abstracto,* but always to *particular* Councils, or rather to their "faith" and witness. Pere Yves Congar has recently published an excellent article on the "Primacy of the first four Ecumenical Councils," and the evidence he has collected is highly instructive.[10] In fact, it was precisely the normative priority of Nicea, Ephesus, and Chalcedon, that is, of their dogmatic ruling, which was felt to be a faithful and adequate expression of the perennial commitment of faith as once delivered unto the Church. Again the stress was not so much on "canonical" authority, but on the truth. It leads us to the most intricate and crucial problem — what are the ultimate *criteria* of the Christian Truth?

Christ: The Criterion of Truth

There is no easy answer to this query. Indeed, there is a very simple answer — *Christ is the Truth.* The source and the criterion of the Christian Truth is the Divine Revelation, in its twofold structure, in its two dispensations. The source

of the Truth is the Word of God. Now, this simple answer
was readily given and commonly accepted in the Ancient
Church, as it may be also gratefully accepted in the divided
Christendom of our own days. Yet, this answer does not solve
the problem. In fact, it has been variously assessed and interpreted, to the point of most radical divergence. It only meant
that the problem was actually shifted a step further. A new
question came to be asked. How was Revelation to be understood? The Early Church had no doubt about the "sufficiency" of the Scriptures, and never tried to go beyond, and
always claimed not to have gone beyond. But already in the
Apostolic age itself the problem of "interpretation" arose
in all its challenging sharpness. What was the guiding hermeneutical principle? At this point there was no other answer
than the appeal to the "faith of the Church," the faith and
kerygma of the Apostles, the Apostolic *paradosis*. The Scripture could be understood only within the Church, as Origen
strongly insisted, and as St. Irenaeus and Tertullian insisted
before him. The appeal to Tradition was actually an appeal
to the mind of the Church, her *phronema*. It was a method
to discover and ascertain the faith as it had been always held,
from the very beginning: *semper creditum*. The *permanence*
of Christian belief was the most conspicuous sign and token
of its truth: no innovations.[11] And this permanence of the
Holy Church's faith could be appropriately demonstrated
by the witnesses from the past. It was for that reason, and
for that purpose, that "the ancients" — οἱ παλαιοί — were
usually invoked and quoted in theological discussions. This
"argument from antiquity," however, had to be used with
certain caution. Occasional references to old times and casual
quotations from old authors could be often ambiguous and
even misleading. This was well understood already at the
time of the great Baptismal controversy in the third century,
and the question about the validity or authority of "ancient
customs" had been formally raised at that time. Already
Tertullian contended that *consuetudines* [customs] in the
Church had to be examined in the light of truth: *Dominus
noster Christus veritatem se, non consuetudinem, cognomin-
avit* [Our Lord Christ designated himself, not as custom but

as truth; *de virginibus velandis,* I.I]. The phrase was taken up by St. Cyprian and was adopted by the Council at Carthage in 256. In fact, "antiquity" as such might happen to be no more than an inveterate error: *nam antiquitas sine veritate vetustas erroris est* [for antiquity without truth is the age old error], in the phrase of St. Cyprian (*epist.* 74.9). St. Augustine also used the same phrase: *In Evangelio Dominus, Ego sum, inquit, veritas. Non dixit, Ego sum consuetudo* [In the Gospel the Lord says—I am the truth. He did not say—I am custom; *de baptismo,* III. 6.9]. "Antiquity" as such was not necessarily a truth, although the Christian truth was intrinsically an "ancient" truth, and "innovations" in the Church had to be resisted. On the other hand, the argument "from tradition" was first used by the heretics, by Gnostics, and it was this usage of theirs that prompted St. Irenaeus to elaborate his own conception of Tradition — in opposition to the false "traditions" of the heretics which were alien to the mind of the Church.[2] The appeal to "antiquity" or "traditions" had to be selective and discriminative. Certain alleged "traditions" were simply wrong and false. One had to detect and to identify the "true Tradition," the authentic Tradition which could be traced back to the authority of the Apostles and be attested and confirmed by an universal *consensio* of Churches. In fact, however, this *consensio* could not be so easily discovered. Certain questions were still open. The main criterion of St. Irenaeus was valid: Tradition — Apostolic and Catholic (or Universal). Origen, in the preface to his *De Principiis,* tried to describe the scope of the existing "agreement" which was to his mind binding and restrictive, and then he quoted a series of important topics which had to be further explored. There was, again, a considerable variety of local traditions, in language and discipline, even within the unbroken communion in faith and *in sacris.* It suffices to recall at this point the Pascal controversy between Rome and the East, in which the whole question of the authority of ancient habits came to the fore. One should also recall the conflicts between Carthage and Rome, and also between Rome and Alexandria, in the third century, and the increasing tension between Alexandria and Antioch which came to its tragic climax, and impass, in the fifth century. Now, in this age of the intense theological controvercy and context, all participating groups used to appeal to tradition and "antiquity." "Chains" of ancient testimonies were compiled on all sides in the dispute. These testimonies had to be carefully scrutinized and examined on a basis more comprehensive that "antiquity" alone. Certain local traditions, liturgical and theological, were finally discarded and disavowed by the overarching authority of an "ecumenical" *consensus*. A sharp confrontation of diverse theological traditions took place already at the Council of Ephesus. The Council was actually split in twain—the "Ecumenical" Council of St. Cyril and Rome and the *conciliabulum* of the Orient. Indeed, the reconciliation was achieved, and yet there was still a tension. The most spectacular instance of condemnation of a theological tradition, of long standing and of considerable, if rather local, renown, was, of course, the dramatic affair of Three Chapters. At this point a question of principle has been raised: to what extent was it fair and legitimate to disavow the faith of those who had died in peace and in communion with the Church? There was a violent debate on this matter, especially in the West, and strong arguments were produced against such retrospective discrimination. Nevertheless, the Chapters were condemned by the Fifth Ecumenical Council. "Antiquity" was overruled by Ecumenical *consensio*, as strained as it probably was.

The Meaning of the Appeal to the Fathers

It has been rightly observed that appeal to "antiquity" was changing its function and character with the course of time. The Apostolic past was still at hand, and within the reach of human memory, in the times of St. Irenaeus or Tertullian. Indeed, St. Irenaeus had heard in his youth the oral instruction of St. Polycarp, the immediate disciple of St. John the Divine. It was only the third generation since Christ! The memory of the Apostolic age was still fresh. The scope of Christian history was brief and limited. The main concern in this early age was with the Apostolic *foundations*, with the *initial delivery* of the *kerygma*. Accordingly, Tradition meant at that time, primarily, the original "delivery" or "deposition." The question of accurate transmission, over a bit more than one century, was comparatively simple, especially in the Churches founded by the Apostles themselves. Full attention was given, of course, to the lists of episcopal succession (cf. St. Irenaeus or Hegesippus), but it was not difficult to compile these lists. The question of "succession," however, appeared to be much more complicated for the subsequent generations, more removed from the Apostolic time. It was but natural, under these new conditions, that emphasis should shift from the question of initial "Apostolicity" to the problem of the preservation of the "deposit." Tradition came to mean "transmission," rather than "delivery." The question of the intermediate links, of "succession" — in the wide and comprehensive sense of the word — became especially urgent. It was the problem of faithful witnesses. It was in this situation that the authority of the Fathers was for the first time formally invoked: they were witnesses of the permanence or identity of the *kerygma,* as transmitted from generation to generation.[13] Apostles *and* Fathers — these two terms were generally and commonly coupled together in the argument from Tradition, as it was used in the Third and Fourth centuries. It was this *double* reference, both to the *origin* and to the unfailing and continuous *preservation,* that warranted the authenticity of belief. On the other hand, Scripture was formally acknowledged and recognized as the ground and foundation of faith, as the Word of God and the Writ of the Spirit. Yet, there was still the problem of right and adequate interpretation. Scripture and Fathers were usually quoted together, that is, *kerygma* and *exegesis,* — ἡ γραφὴ καὶ οἱ πατέρες.

The reference, or even a direct appeal, *"to the Fathers"* was a distinctive and salient note of theological research and discussion in the period of the great General or Ecumenical Councils, beginning with that of Nicea. The term has never been formally defined. It was used, occasionally and sporadically, already by early ecclesiastical writers. Often it simply denoted Christian teachers and leaders of previous generations. It was gradually becoming a title for the bishops, in so far as they were appointed teachers and witnesses of faith. Later the title was applied specifically to bishops in Councils. The common element in all these cases was the teaching office or task. "Fathers" were those who transmitted and propagated the right doctrine, the teaching of the Apostles, who were guides and masters in Christian instruction and catechesis. In this sense it was emphatically applied to great Christian writers. It must be kept in mind that the main, if not also the only, manual of faith and doctrine was, in the Ancient Church, precisely the Holy Writ. And for that reason the renowned interpreters of Scripture were regarded as "Fathers" in an eminent sense.[14] "Fathers" were teachers, first of all, — *doctores*, διδάσκαλοι. And they were teachers in so far as they were witnesses, *testes*. These two functions must be distinguished, and yet they are most intimately intertwined. "Teaching" was an Apostolic task: "teach all nations." And it was in this commission that their "authority" was rooted: it was, in fact, the authority to bear witness. Two major points must be made in this connection. *First,* the phrase "the Fathers of the Church" has actually an obvious *restrictive* accent: they were acting not just as individuals, but rather as *viri ecclesiastici* (the favourite expression of Origen), on behalf and in the name of the Church. They were spokesmen for the Church, expositors of her faith, keepers of her Tradition, witnesses of truth and faith, — *magistri probabiles,* in the phrase of St. Vincent. And in that was their "authority" grounded.[15] It leads us back to the concept of "representation." The late G. L. Prestige has rightly observed:

> The creeds of the Church grew out of the teaching of the Church: the general effect of heresy was rather to force old creeds to be tightened up than to cause fresh creeds to be constructed. Thus the most famous and most crucial of all creeds, that of Nicea, was only a new edition of an existing Palestinian confession. And a further important fact always ought to be remembered. *The real intellectual work, the vital interpretative thought, was not contributed by the Councils that promulgated the creeds, but by the theological teachers who supplied and explained the formulae which the Councils adopted. The teaching of Nicea, which finally commended itself, represented the views of intellectual giants work-*

ing for a hundred years before and for fifty years after the actual meeting of the Council.[16]

The Fathers were true inspirers of the Councils, while being present and *in absentia,* and also often after they have gone to Eternal Rest. For that reason, and in this sense, the Councils used to emphasize that they were "following the Holy Fathers" — ἑπόμενοι τοῖς ἁγίοις πατράσιν, as Chalcedon has said. *Secondly,* it was precisely the *consensus patrum* which was authoritative and binding, and not their private opinions or views, although even they should not be hastily dismissed. Again, this *consensus* was much more than just an empirical agreement of individuals. The true and authentic *consensus* was that which reflected the mind of the Catholic and Universal Church — τὸ ἐκκλησιαστικὸν φρόνη-μα.[17] It was that kind of *consensus* to which St. Irenaeus was referring when he contended that neither a special "ability," nor a "deficiency" in speech of individual leaders in the Churches could affect the identity of their witness, since the "power of tradition" — *virtus traditionis*—was always and everywhere the same (*adv. haeres.* I. 10.2). The preaching of the Church is always identical: *constans et aequaliter perseverans* (ibid., III. 24.1). The true *consensus* is that which manifests and discloses this perennial identity of the Church's faith — *aequaliter perseverans.*[18]

The teaching *authority* of the Ecumenical Councils is grounded in the *infallibility* of the Church. The ultimate "authority" is vested in the Church which is for ever the Pillar and the Foundation of Truth. It is not primarily a *canonical* authority, in the formal and specific sense of the term, although canonical strictures or sanctions may be appended to conciliar decisions on matters of faith. It is a *charismatic* authority, grounded in the assistance of the Spirit: *for it seemed good to the Holy Spirit, and to us.*

CHAPTER VII

St. Gregory Palamas and the Tradition
of the Fathers

Following the Fathers

"FOLLOWING THE HOLY FATHERS" . . . It was usual in the Ancient Church to introduce doctrinal statements by phrases like this. The Decree of Chalcedon opens precisely with these very words. The Seventh Ecumenical Council introduces its decision concerning the Holy Icons in a more elaborate way: *"Following the Divinely inspired teaching of the Holy Fathers and the Tradition of the Catholic Church."* The *didaskalia* of the Fathers is the formal and normative term of reference.

Now, this was much more than just an "appeal to antiquity." Indeed, the Church always stresses the permanence of her faith through the ages, from the very beginning. This identity, since the Apostolic times, is the most conspicuous sign and token of right faith—always the same. Yet, "antiquity" by itself is not an adequate proof of the true faith. Moreover, the Christian message was obviously a striking "novelty" for the "ancient world," and, indeed, a call to radical "renovation." The "Old" has passed away, and everything has been "made New." On the other hand, heresies could also appeal to the past and invoke the authority of

---

"St. Gregory Palamas and the Tradition of the Fathers" appeared in *The Greek Orthodox Theological Review* (Winter, 1959—1960; V, 2). Copyright by *The Greek Orthodox Theological Review* and reprinted with permission.

certain "traditions." In fact, heresies were often lingering in the past.[1] Archaic formulas can often be dangerously misleading. Vincent of Lerins himself was fully aware of this danger. It would suffice to quote this pathetic passage of his: "And now, what an amazing reversal of the situation! the authors of the same opinion are adjudged to be catholics, but the followers—heretics; the masters are absolved, the disciples are condemned; the writers of the books will be children of the Kingdom, their followers will go to Gehenna" (*Commonitorium,* cap. 6). Vincent had in mind, of course, St. Cyprian and the Donatists. St. Cyprian himself faced the same situation. "Antiquity" as such may happen to be just an inveterate prejudice: *nam antiquitas sine veritate vetustas erroris est* (*Epist.* 74). It is to say—"old customs" as such do not guarantee the truth. "Truth" is not just a "habit."

The true tradition is only the tradition of truth, *traditio veritatis.* This tradition, according of St. Irenaeus, is grounded in, and secured by, that *charisma veritatis certum* [secure charisma of truth], which has been "deposited" in the Church from the very beginning and has been preserved by the uninterrupted succession of episcopal ministry. "Tradition" in the Church is not a continuity of human memory, or a permanence of rites and habits. It is a living tradition—*depositum juvenescens,* in the phrase of St. Irenaeus. Accordingly, it cannot be counted inter *mortuas regulas* [among dead rules]. Ultimately, tradition is a continuity of the abiding presence of the Holy Spirit in the Church, a continuity of Divine guidance and illumination. The Church is not bound by the "letter." Rather, she is constantly moved forth by the "Spirit." The same Spirit, the Spirit of Truth, which "spake through the Prophets," which guided the Apostles, is still continuously guiding the Church into the fuller comprehension and understanding of the Divine truth, from glory to glory.

"Following the Holy Fathers" . . . This is not a reference to some abstract tradition, in formulas and propositions. It is primarily an appeal to holy witnesses. Indeed, we appeal to the Apostles, and not just to an abstract "Apostolicity." In the similar manner do we refer to the Fathers. The witness

of the Fathers belongs, intrinsically and integrally, to the very structure of Orthodox belief. The Church is equally committed to the *kerygma* of the Apostles and to the *dogma* of the Fathers. We may quote at this point an admirable ancient hymn (probably, from the pen of St. Romanus the Melode). "Preserving the kerygma of the Apostles and the dogmas of the Fathers, the Church has sealed the one faith and wearing the tunic of truth she shapes rightly the brocade of heavenly theology and praises the great mystery of piety.'"

The Mind of the Fathers

The Church is "Apostolic" indeed. But the Church is also "Patristic." She is intrinsically "the Church of the Fathers." These two "notes" cannot be separated. Only by being "Patristic" is the Church truly "Apostolic." The witness of the Fathers is much more than simply a historic feature, a voice from the past. Let us quote another hymn— from the office of the Three Hierarchs. "By the word of knowledge you have composed the dogmas which the fishermen have established first in simple words, in knowledge by the power of the Spirit, for thus our simple piety had to acquire composition." There are, as it were, two basic stages in the proclamation of the Christian faith. "Our simple faith had to acquire composition." There was an inner urge, an inner logic, an internal necessity, in this transition—from *kerygma* to *dogma*. Indeed, the teaching of the Fathers, and the dogma of the Church, are still the same "simple message" which has been once delivered and deposited, once for ever, by the Apostles. But now it is, as it were, properly and fully articulated. The Apostolic preaching is kept alive in the Church, not only merely preserved. In this sense, the teaching of the Fathers is a permanent category of Christian existence, a constant and ultimate measure and criterion of right faith. Fathers are not only witnesses of the old faith, *testes antiquitatis*. They are rather witnesses of the true faith, *testes veritatis*. "The mind of the Fathers" is an intrinsic term of reference in Orthodox theology, no less than the word of Holy Scripture, and indeed never separated from it.

As it has been well said, "the Catholic Church of all ages is not merely a daughter of the Church of the Fathers— *she is and remains the Church of the Fathers.*"[3]

The Existential Character of Patristic Theology

The main distinctive mark of Patristic theology was its "existential" character, if we may use this current neologism. The Fathers theologized, as St. Gregory of Nazianzus put it, "in the manner of the Apostles, not in that of Aristotle"— ἀλιευτικῶς, οὐκ ἀριστοτελικῶς (*Hom.* 23. 12). Their theology was still a "message," a *kerygma.* Their theology was still "kerygmatic theology," even if it was often logically arranged and supplied with intellectual arguments. The ultimate reference was still to the vision of faith, to spiritual knowledge and experience. Apart from life in Christ theology carries no conviction and, if separated from the life of faith, theology may degenerate into empty dialectics, a vain *polylogia,* without any spiritual consequence. Patristic theology was existentially rooted in the decisive commitment of faith. It was not a self-explanatory "discipline" which could be presented argumentatively, that is ἀριστοτελικῶς, without any prior spiritual engagement. In the age of theological strife and incessant debates, the great Cappadocian Fathers formally protested against the use of dialectics, of "Aristotelian syllogisms," and endeavoured to refer theology back to the vision of faith. Patristic theology could be only "preached" or "proclaimed"—preached from the pulpit, proclaimed also in the words of prayer and in the sacred rites, and indeed manifested in the total structure of Christian life. Theology of this kind can never be separated from the life of prayer and from the exercise of virtue. "The climax of purity is the beginning of theology," as St. John the Klimakos puts it: Τέλος δὲ ἁγνείας ὑπόθεσις θεολογίας (*Scala Paradisi,* grade 30).

On the other hand, theology of this type is always, as it were, "propaideutic," since its ultimate aim and purpose is to ascertain and to acknowledge the Mystery of the Living God, and indeed to bear witness to it, in word and deed.

"Theology" is not an end in itself. It is always but a way. Theology, and even the "dogmas," present no more than an "intellectual contour" of the revealed truth, and a "noetic" testimony to it. Only in the act of faith is this "contour" filled with content. Christological formulas are fully meaningful only for those who have encountered the Living Christ, and have received and acknowledged Him as God and Saviour, and are dwelling by faith in Him, in His body, the Church. In this sense, theology is never a self-explanatory discipline. It is constantly appealing to the *vision of faith*. "What we have seen and have heard we announce to you." Apart from this "announcement" theological formulas are empty and of no consequence. For the same reason these formulas can never be taken "abstractly," that is, out of total context of belief. It is misleading to single out particular statements of the Fathers and to detach them from the total perspective in which they have been actually uttered, just as it is misleading to manipulate with detached quotations from the Scripture. It is a dangerous habit *"to quote"* the Fathers, that is, their isolated sayings and phrases, outside of that concrete setting in which only they have their full and proper meaning and are truly alive. *"To follow"* the Fathers does *not* mean just *"to quote"* them. "To follow" the Fathers means to acquire their "mind," their *phronema*.

The Meaning of the "Age" of the Fathers

Now, we have reached the crucial point. The name of "Church Fathers" is usually restricted to *the teachers of the Ancient Church*. And it is currently assumed that their authority depends upon their "antiquity," upon their comparative nearness to the "Primitive Church," to the initial "Age" of the Church. Already St. Jerome had to contest this idea. Indeed, there was no decrease of "authority," and no decrease in the immediacy of spiritual competence and knowledge, in the course of Christian history. In fact, however, this idea of "decrease" has strongly affected our modern theological thinking. In fact, it is too often assumed, consciously or unconsciously, that the Early Church was, as it were, closer to the spring of truth. As an admission of our own failure and inadequacy, as an act of humble self-criticism, such an assumption is sound and helpful. *But it is dangerous to make of it the starting point or basis of our "theology of Church history,"* or even of our theology of the Church. Indeed, the Age of the Apostles should retain its unique position. Yet, it was just a beginning. It is widely assumed that the "Age of the Fathers" has also ended, and accordingly it is regarded just as an ancient formation, "antiquated" in a sense and "archaic." The limit of the "Patristic Age" is variously defined. It is usual to regard St. John of Damascus as the "last Father" in the East, and St. Gregory the Dialogos or Isidore of Seville as "the last" in the West. This periodization has been justly contested in recent times. Should not, for instance, St. Theodore of Studium, at least, be included among "the Fathers"? Mabillon has suggested that Bernard of Clairvaux, the Doctor mellifluous, was "the last of the Fathers, and surely not unequal to the earlier ones."[4] Actually, it is more than a question of periodization. *From the Western point of view "the Age of the Fathers" has been succeeded, and indeed superseded, by "the Age of the Schoolmen,"* which was an essential step forward. Since the rise of Scholasticism "Patristic theology" has been antiquated, has become actually a "past age," a kind of archaic prelude. This point of view, legitimate for the West, has been, most unfortunately, accepted also by many in the East, blindly and uncritically. Accordingly, one has to face the alternative. *Either* one has to regret the "backwardness" of the East which never developed any "Scholasticism" of its own. *Or* one should retire into the "Ancient Age," in a more or less archeological manner, and practice what has been wittily described recently as a "theology of repetition." The latter, in fact, is just a peculiar form of imitative "scholasticism."

Now, it is not seldom suggested that, probably, "the Age of the Fathers" has ended much earlier than St. John of Damascus. Very often one does not proceed further than the Age of Justinian, or even already the Council of Chalcedon. Was not Leontius of Byzantium already "the first of the Scholastics"? Psychologically, this attitude is quite comprehensible, although it cannot be theologically justified. Indeed, the Fathers of the Fourth century are much more impressive, and their unique greatness cannot be denied. Yet, the Church remained fully alive also after Nicea and Chalcedon. The current overemphasis on the "first five centuries" dangerously distorts theological vision, and prevents the right understanding of the Chalcedonian dogma itself. The decree of the Sixth Ecumenical Council is often regarded as a kind of an "appendix" to Chalcedon, interesting only for theological specialists, and the great figure of St. Maximus the Confessor is almost completely ignored. Accordingly, the theological significance of the Seventh Ecumenical Council is dangerously obscured, and one is left to wonder, why the Feast of Orthodoxy should be related to the commemoration of the Church's victory over the Iconoclasts. Was it not just a "ritualistic controversy"? We often forget that the famous formula of the *Consensus quinque-saecularis* [agreement of five centuries], that is, actually, up to Chalcedon, was a Protestant formula, and reflected a peculiar Protestant "theology of history." It was a *restrictive* formula, as much as it seemed to be too inclusive to those who wanted to be secluded in the Apostolic Age. The point is, however, that the current Eastern formula of "the Seven Ecumenical Councils" is hardly much better, if it tends, as it usually does, *to restrict* or to limit the Church's spiritual authority to the first eight centuries, as if "the Golden Age" of Christianity has already passed and we are now, probably, already in an Iron Age, much lower on the scale of spiritual vigour and authority. Our theological thinking has been dangerously affected by *the pattern of decay,* adopted for the interpretation of Christian history in the West since the Reformation. The fullness of the Church was then interpreted in a static manner, and the attitude to Antiquity has been accordingly distorted and misconstrued. After all, it does not make much difference, whether we *restrict* the normative authority of the Church to one century, or to five, or to eight. *There should be no restriction at all.* Consequently, there is no room for any "theology of repetition." The Church is still fully authoritative as she has been in the ages past, since the Spirit of Truth quickens her now no less effectively as in the ancient times.

The Legacy of Byzantine Theology

One of the immediate results of our careless periodization is that we simply ignore *the legacy of Byzantine theology.* We are prepared, now more than only a few decades ago, to admit the perennial authority of "the Fathers," especially since the revival of Patristic studies in the West. But we still tend to limit the scope of admission, and obviously "Byzantine theologians" are not readily counted among the "Fathers." We are inclined to discriminate rather rigidly between "Patristics"—in a more or less narrow sense—and "Byzantinism." We are still inclined to regard "Byzantinism" as an inferior sequel to the Patristic Age. We have still doubts about its normative relevance for theological thinking. Now, Byzantine theology was much more than just a "repetition" of Patristic theology, nor was that which was new in it of an inferior quality in comparison with "Christian Antiquity." Indeed, *Byzantine theology was an organic continuation of the Patristic Age.* Was there any break? Has the *ethos* of the Eastern Orthodox Church been ever changed, at a certain historic point or date, which, however, has never been unanimously identified, so that the "later" development was of lesser authority and importance, if of any? This admission seems to be silently implied in the *restrictive* commitment to the *Seven* Ecumenical Councils. Then, St. Symeon the New Theologian and St. Gregory Palamas are simply left out, and the great Hesychast Councils of the fourteenth century are ignored and forgotten. What is their position and authority in the Church?

Now, in fact, St. Symeon and St. Gregory are still authoritative masters and inspirers of all those who, in the Orthodox Church, are striving after perfection, and are living the life of prayer and contemplation, whether in the surviving monastic communities, or in the solitude of the desert, and even in the world. These faithful people are not aware of any alleged "break" between "Patristics" and

"Byzantinism." The *Philokalia,* this great encyclopaedia of Eastern piety, which includes writings of many centuries, is, in our own days, increasingly becoming the manual of guidance and instruction for all those who are eager *to practice Orthodoxy* in our contemporary situation. The authority of its compiler, St. Nicodemus of the Holy Mount, has been recently recognized and enhanced by his formal canonization in the Church. In this sense, we are bound to say, "the Age of the Fathers" still continues in "the Worshipping Church." Should it not continue also in our theological pursuit and study, research and instruction? Should we not recover "the mind of the Fathers" also in our theological thinking and teaching? To recover it, indeed, not as an archaic manner or pose, and not just as a venerable relic, but as *an existential attitude,* as *a spiritual orientation.* Only in this way can our theology be reintegrated into the fullness of our Christian existence. It is not enough to keep a "Byzantine Liturgy," as we do, to restore Byzantine iconography and Byzantine music, as we are still reluctant to do consistently, and to practice certain Byzantine modes of devotion. One has to go to the very roots of this traditional "piety," and to recover the "Patristic mind." Otherwise we may be in danger of being inwardly split—as many in our midst actually are—between the "traditional" forms of "piety" and a very untraditional habit of theological thinking. It is a real danger. As "worshippers" we are still in "the tradition of the Fathers." Should we not stand, conscientiously and avowedly, in the same tradition also as "theologians," as witnesses and teachers of Orthodoxy? Can we retain our integrity in any other way?

St. Gregory Palamas and Theosis

All these preliminary considerations are highly relevant for our immediate purpose. What is the theological legacy of St. Gregory Palamas? St. Gregory was not a speculative theologian. He was a monk and a bishop. He was not concerned about abstract problems of philosophy, although he was well trained in this field too. He was concerned solely with problems of Christian existence. As a theologian, he was simply an interpreter of the spiritual experience of the Church. Almost all his writings, except probably his homilies, were occasional writings. He was wrestling with the problems of his own time. And it was a critical time, an age of controversy and anxiety. Indeed, it was also an age of spiritual renewal.

St. Gregory was suspected of subversive innovations by his enemies in his own time. This charge is still maintained against him in the West. In fact, however, St. Gregory was deeply rooted in tradition. It is not difficult to trace most of his views and motives back to the Cappadocian Fathers and to St. Maximus the Confessor, who was, by the way, one of the most popular masters of Byzantine thought and devotion. Indeed, St. Gregory was also intimately acquainted with the writings of Pseudo-Dionysius. He was rooted in the tradition. *Yet, in no sense was his theology just a "theology of repetition." It was a creative extension of ancient tradition. Its starting point was Life in Christ.*

Of all themes of St. Gregory's theology let us single out but one, the crucial one, and the most controversial. What is the basic character of Christian existence? The ultimate aim and purpose of human life was defined in the Patristic tradition as θέωσις [theosis; divinization]. The term is rather offensive for the modern ear. It cannot be adequately rendered in any modern language, nor even in Latin. Even in Greek it is rather heavy and pretentious. Indeed, it is a daring word. The meaning of the word is, however, simple and lucid. It was one of the crucial terms in the Patristic vocabulary. It would suffice to quote at this point but St. Athanasius. Γέγονεν γὰρ ἄνθρωπος, ἵν' ἡμᾶς ἐν ἑαυτῷ θεοποιήσῃ. [He became man in order to divinize us in Himself (*Ad Adelphium* 4)]. Αὐτὸς γὰρ ἐνηνθρώπησεν, ἵνα ἡμεῖς θεοποιηθῶμεν. [He became man in order that we might be divinized (*De Incarnatione* 54)]. St. Athanasius actually resumes here the favourite idea of St. Irenaeus: *qui propter immensam dilectionem suam factus est quod sumus nos, uti nos perficeret esse quod est ipse.* [Who, through his immense love became what we are, that He might bring us to be even what He is Himself (*Adv. Haeres.* V, Praefatio)]. It was the common conviction of the Greek Fathers. One can quote at length St. Gregory of Nazianzus. St. Gregory of Nyssa, St. Cyril of Alexandria, St. Maximus, and indeed St. Symeon the New Theologian. Man ever remains what he is, that is—creature. But he is promised and granted, in Christ Jesus, the Word become man, an intimate sharing in what is Divine: Life Everlasting and incorruptible. The main characteristic of *theosis* is, according to the Fathers, precisely "immortality" or "incorruption." For God alone "has immortality"—ὁ μόνος ἔχων ἀθανασίαν (I Tim. 6:16). But man now is admitted into an intimate "communion" with God, through Christ and by the power of the Holy Spirit. And this is much more than just a "moral" communion, and much more than just a human perfection. Only the word *theosis* can render adequately the uniqueness of the promise and offer. *The term theosis is indeed quite embarrassing, if we would think in "ontological" categories.* Indeed, man simply cannot "become" god. But the Fathers were thinking in "personal" terms, and the mystery of *personal* communion was involved at this point. *Theosis meant a personal encounter.* It is that intimate intercourse of man with God, in which the whole of human existence is, as it were, permeated by the Divine Presence.[5]

Yet, the problem remains: How can even this intercourse be compatible with the Divine Transcendance? And this is the crucial point. Does man really encounter God, in this present life on earth? Does man encounter God, truly and verily, in his present life of prayer? Or, is there no more than an *actio in distans?* The common claim of the Eastern Fathers was that in his devotional ascent man actually encounters God and beholds His eternal Glory. Now, how is it possible, if God "abides in the light unapproachable"? The paradox was especially sharp in the Eastern theology, which has been always committed to the belief that God was absolutely "incomprehensible"—ἀκατάληπτος—and unknowable in His nature or essence.

This conviction was powerfully expressed by the Cappadocian Fathers, especially in their struggle against Eunomius, and also by St. John Chrysostom, in his magnificent discourses Περὶ ᾿Ακαταλήπτου. *Thus, if God is absolutely "unapproachable" in His essence, and accordingly His essence simply cannot be "communicated," how can theosis be possible at all?* "One insults God who seeks to apprehend His essential being," says Chrysostom. Already in St. Athanasius we find a clear distinction between God's very "essence" and His powers and bounty: Καὶ ἐν πᾶσι μέν ἐστι κατὰ τὴν ἑαυτοῦ ἀγαθότητα, ἔξω δὲ τῶν πάντων πάλιν ἐστι κατὰ τὴν ἰδίαν φύσιν. [He is in everything by his love, but outside of everything by his own nature (*De Decretis* II)]. The same conception was carefully elaborated by the Cappadocians. The "essence of God" is absolutely inaccessible to man, says St. Basil (*Adv. Eunomium* 1:14). We know God only *in* His actions, and by His actions: ῾Ημεῖς δὲ ἐκ μὲν τῶν ἐνεργειῶν γνωρίζειν λέγομεν τὸν Θεὸν ἡμῶν, τῇ δὲ οὐσίᾳ προσεγγίζειν οὐχ ὑπισχνούμεθα αἱ μὲν γὰρ ἐνέργειαι αὐτοῦ πρὸς ἡμᾶς καταβαίνουσιν, ἡ δὲ οὐσία αὐτοῦ μένει ἀπρόσιτος. [We say that we know our God from his energies (activities), but we do not profess to approach his essence—for his energies descend to us, but his essence remains inaccessible (*Epist.* 234, ad Amphilochium)]. Yet, it is a true knowledge, not just a conjecture or deduction: αἱ ἐνέργειαι αὐτοῦ πρὸς ἡμᾶς καταβαίνουσιν. In the phrase of St. John of Damascus, these actions or "energies" of God are the true revelation of God Himself: ἡ θεία ἔλλαμψις καὶ ἐνέργεια (*De Fide Orth.* I: 14). It is *a real presence,* and not merely a certain *praesentia operativa, sicut agens adest ei in quod agit* [as the actor is present in the thing in which he acts]. This mysterious mode of Divine Presence, in spite of the absolute transcendence of the Divine Essence, passes all understanding. But it is no less certain for that reason.

St. Gregory Palamas stands in an ancient tradition at this point. In His "energies" the Unapproachable God mysteriously approaches man. And this Divine move effects encounter: πρόοδος εἰς τὰ ἔξω, in the phrase of St. Maximus (*Scholia in De Div. Nom.*, I: 5).

St. Gregory begins with the distinction between "grace" and "essence": ἡ θεία καὶ θεοποιὸς ἔλλαμψις καὶ χάρις οὐκ οὐσία, ἀλλ᾿ ἐνέργεια ἐστι Θεοῦ [the Divine and Divinizing illumination and grace is not the essence, but the energy of God; *Capita Phys., Theol., etc.*, 68—9]. This basic distinction was formally accepted and elaborated at the Great Councils in Constantinople, 1341 and 1351. Those who would deny this distinction were anathematized and excommunicated. The anathematisms of the council of 1351 were included in the rite for the Sunday of Orthodoxy, in the Triodion. Orthodox theologians are bound by this decision. The essence of God is absolutely ἀμεθεκτή [incommunicable]. The source and the power of human *theosis* is not the Divine essence, but the "Grace of God": θεοποιὸς ἐνέργεια, ἧς τὰ μετέχοντα θεοῦνται, θεία τις ἐστι χάρις, ἀλλ᾿ οὐχ ἡ φύσις τοῦ Θεοῦ [the divinizing energy, by participation of which one is divinized, is a divine grace, but in no way the essence of God; *ibid.* 92—3]. Χάρις is not identical with the οὐσία. It is θεία καὶ ἄκτιστος χάρις καὶ ἐνέργεια [Divine and uncreated Grace and Energy; *ibid.*, 69]. This distinction, however, does not imply or effect division or separation. Nor is it just an "accident," οὔτε συμβεβηκότος (*ibid.*, 127). Energies "proceed" from God and manifest His own Being. The term προϊέναι [proceed] simply suggests διάκρισιν [distinction], but not a division: εἰ καὶ διενήνοχε τῆς φύσεως, οὐ διασπᾶται ἡ τοῦ Πνεύματος χάρις [the grace of the Spirit is different from the Substance, and yet not separated from it; *Theophanes*, p. 940].

Actually the whole teaching of St. Gregory presupposes the action of the Personal God. God moves toward man and embraces him by His own "grace" and action, without leaving that φῶς ἀπρόσιτον [light unapproachable], in which He eternally abides. The ultimate purpose of St. Gregory's theological teaching was to defend the reality of Christian experience. *Salvation is more than forgiveness. It is a genuine renewal of man.* And this renewal is effected not by the discharge, or release, of certain natural energies implied in man's own creaturely being, but by the "energies" of God Himself, who thereby encounters and encompasses man, and admits him into communion with Himself. *In fact, the teaching of St. Gregory affects the whole system of theology, the whole body of Christian doctrine. It starts with the clear distinction between "nature" and "will" of God.* This distinction was also characteristic of the Eastern tradition, at least since St. Athanasius. It may be asked at this point: Is this distinction compatible with the "simplicity" of God? Should we not rather regard all these distinctions as merely logical conjectures, necessary for us, but ultimately without any ontological significance? As a matter of fact, St. Gregory Palamas was attacked by his opponents precisely from that point of view. God's Being is simple, and in Him even all attributes coincide. Already St. Augustine diverged at this point from the Eastern tradition. Under Augustinian presuppositions the teaching of St. Gregory is unacceptable and absurd. St. Gregory himself anticipated the width of implications of his basic distinction. If one does not accept it, he argued, then it would be impossible to discern clearly between the "generation" of the Son and "creation" of the world, both being the acts of essence, and this would lead to utter confusion in the Trinitarian doctrine. St. Gregory was quite formal at that point.

> If according to the delirious opponents and those who agree with them, the Divine energy in no way differs from the Divine essence, then the act of creating, which belongs to the will, will in no way differ from generation (γεννᾶν) and procession (ἐκπορεύειν), which belong to the essence. If to create is no different from generation and procession, then the creatures will in no way differ from the Begotten (γεννήματος) and the Projected (προβλή-ματος). If such is the case according to them, then both the Son of God and the Holy Spirit will be no different from creatures, and the creatures will all be both the begotten (γεννήματα) and the projected (προβλήματα) of God the Father, and creation will be deified and God will be arrayed with the creatures. For this reason the venerable Cyril, showing the difference between God's essence and energy, says that to generate belongs to the Divine nature, whereas to create belongs to His Divine energy. This he shows clearly saying, "nature and energy are not the same." If the Divine essence in no way differs from the Divine energy, then to beget (γεννᾶν) and to project (ἐκπορεύειν) will in no way

differ from creating (ποιεῖν). God the Father creates by the Son and in the Holy Spirit. Thus He also begets and projects by the Son and in the Holy Spirit, according to the opinion of the opponents and those who agree with them. (*Capita* 96 and 97.)

St. Gregory quotes St. Cyril of Alexandria. But St. Cyril at this point was simply repeating St. Athanasius. St. Athanasius, in his refutation of Arianism, formally stressed the ultimate difference between οὐσία [essence] or φύσις [substance], on the one hand, and the βούλησις [will], on the other. God exists, and then He also acts. There is a certain "necessity" in the Divine Being, indeed not a necessity of compulsion, and no *fatum,* but a necessity of being itself. God simply is what He is. But God's will is eminently free. He in no sense is necessitated to do what He does. Thus γέννησις [generation] is always κατὰ φύσιν [according to essence], but creation is a βουλήσεως ἔργον [energy of the will] (Contra Arianos III. 64—6). These two dimensions, that of being and that of acting, are different, and must be clearly distinguished. Of course, this distinction in no way compromises the "Divine simplicity." Yet, it is a real distinction, and not just a logical device. St. Gregory was fully aware of the crucial importance of this distinction. At this point he was a true successor of the great Athanasius and of the Cappadocian hierarchs.

It has been recently suggested that the theology of St. Gregory, should be described in modern terms as an "existentialist theology." Indeed, it differed radically from modern conceptions which are currently denoted by this label. Yet, in any case, St. Gregory was definitely opposed to all kinds of "essentialist theologies" which fail to account for God's freedom, for the dynamism of God's will, for the reality of Divine action. St. Gregory would trace this trend back to Origen. It was the predicament of the Greek impersonalist metaphysics. If there is any room for Christian metaphysics at all, it must be a metaphysics of persons. The starting point of St. Gregory's theology was *the history of salvation*: on the larger scale, the Biblical story, which consisted of Divine acts, culminating in the Incarnation of the Word and His glorification through the Cross and Resurrection; on the smaller scale, the story of the Christian man, striving after perfection, and ascending step by step, till he encounters God in the vision of His glory. It was usual to describe the theology of St. Irenaeus as a "theology of facts." With no lesser justification we may describe also the theology of St. Gregory Palamas as a "theology of facts."

In our own time, we are coming more and more to the conviction that "theology of facts" is the only sound Orthodox theology. It is Biblical. It is Patristic. It is in complete conformity with the mind of the Church.

In this connection we may regard St. Gregory Palamas as our guide and teacher, in our endeavour to theologize from the heart of the Church.

Notes

CHAPTER III

[1]Jn. vii. 39.
[2]Rom. viii. 15.
[3]Adv. haeres. iii. 10, 2.
[4]Coloss. iii. 3.
[5]I Cor. xv. 45.
[6]I Cor. xv. 20—22.
[7]Eph. ii. 4—6.
[8]Eph. i. 23.
[9]In Ephes. Hom. 3, 2 (Migne, P.G. Ixii. c. 26).
[10]Explan. of Ep. to Ephes. M. 1893, 2. pp. 93—94. For the same point of view, cf. the late Very Rev. J. Armitage Robinson, *St. Paul's Epistle to the Ephesians*, pp. 44—45, I. 403; short ed. pp. 57—60.
[11]Eph. ii. 16.
[12]Col. ii. 19.
[13]Eph. iv. 3.
[14]Jn. xvii. 21—23.
[15]Lk. xviii. 8.
[16]*Opinions and Statements of Philaret, Metropolitan of Moscow, concerning the Orthodox Church in the East* (St. Petersburg, 1886), p. 53.
[17]Ignat. Smyrn. viii. 2.
[18]Mt. xviii. 19—20.
[19]Catech. xviii. 23. (Migne, P.G. xxxiii. c. 1044).
[20]Cf. Pierre Batiffol, *Le Catholicisme de St. Augustin*, I., (Paris, 1920), p. 212.—"Rappelons que le nom 'catholique' a servi à qualifier la Grande Eglise par opposition aux hérétiques . . . Le nom est vraisemblablement de création populaire et apparait en Orient au second siècle. Les *tractatores* du IV. siècle, qui lui cherchent une signification étymologique et savante, veulent y voir l'expression soit de la perfection intégrale de la foi de l'Eglise, soit du fait que l'Eglise ne fait pas acception de personnes de rang, du culture, soit enfin et surtout du fait que l'Eglise est repandue dans le monde entier d'une extrémité à l'autre. Augustin ne veut connaître que ce dernier sens." Cp. also Bishop Lightfoot, in his edition of *St. Ignatius*, v. II. (London, 1889), p. 319. *Note ad loc.*

The history of the Christian and pre-Christian use of the terms ἐκκλησία καθολική and καθολικὸς generally in various settings deserves careful study; apparently there have been no special investigations on the subject. In Russian, reference may be made to the very valuable, though not exhaustive or faultless, article of the late Professor M. D. Muretov in the supplement to his book *Ancient Jewish Prayers ascribed to St. Peter*

(Sergiev Posad, 1905). See also Bishop Lightfoot, *St. Ignatius,* v. II. (London, 1889), p. 310 (note).

[21]Acts iv. 32.

[22]Jn. xvii. 23.

[23]I Cor. xii. 13.

[24]St. John Chrysostom., *In Eph. hom.* XI. 1. (Migne, P.G. lxii., c. 79).

[25]In I Cor. hom. 33, 3. (Migne, P.G. lxi. c. 280).

[26]I Peter ii. 5.

[27]*Hermas,* Vis. III. 2. 6, 8.

[28]For Patristic quotations very well arranged and explained, see E. Mersch, S.J., *Le Corps Mystique du Christ, Etudes de Théologie Historique,* t. I—II (Louvain, 1933).

[29]Archbishop Antony (Khrapovitsky), The Moral Idea of the Dogma of the Church, *Works,* Vol. II., pp. 17—18. (St. Petersburg, 1911).

[30]*Ibid.,* The Moral Idea of the Dogma of the Holy Trinity, p. 65.

[31]*Russia and the English Church,* p. 198.

[32]*Adv. haeres,* i. 10, 2.

[33]*Ibid.,* iv. 26. 2.

[34]Very Rev. W. R. Inge, *The Platonic Tradition in English Religious Thought* (1926), p. 27.

[35]B. M. Melioransky, Lectures on the History of Ancient Christian Churches. *The Pilgrim* (Russian), 1910, 6, p. 931.

[36]I Tim. iii. 15.

[37]S. Paulin. Nolan, epist. XXIII., 25 (*M.L.* LXI., col. 281).

[38]For some more details cp. my articles: "The Work of the Holy Spirit in Revelation," *The Christian East,* V. XIII., No. 2 (1932), and "The Sacrament of Pentecost," *The Journal of the Fellowship of St. Alban and St. Sergius,* No. 23 (March, 1934).

[39]Mt. xviii. 20.

CHAPTER IV

[1]Robert Grosche, *Pilgernde Kirche* (Freiburg im Breisgau, 1938), p. 27.

[2]Sergius Bulgakov, *The Orthodox Church* (1935), p. 12; Stefan Zankow, *Das Orthodoxe Christentum des Ostens* (Berlin 1928), p. 65; English translation by Dr. Lowrie, 1929, p. 6gf.

[3]See M. D. Koster, *Ecclesiologie im Werden* (Paderborn 1940).

[4]Luke xii, 32 *"little flock"* seems to mean precisely the "remnant," reconstituted and redeemed, and reconsecrated.

[5]See Luke vi, 13: "whom also *he named apostles."*

[6]Cf. St. Gregory of Nyssa, *De oratione Dominica,* 3 (MG, XLIV, c. 115f.-1160).

[7]S. Athan. Alex., *Epist. I ad Seraponiem* (MG, XXVI. 576).

[8]St. John Chrysostom, in *Coloss. hom. VII* (MG, LXII, 375).

[9]St. John Chrysostom in *Ephes. hom. III* (MG, LXII, 29).

[10]St. Augustine in *Evangelium Joannis tract, XXI,* 8 (ML., XXXV, 1568); cf. St. John Chrysostom in *I Cor. hom. XXX* (MG, LXI, 279-283).

[11]St. Augustine in *Ev. Joannis tr.* (ML, XXVIII, 1622).

¹²St. Augustine in *Ps. CXXVII*, 3 (ML, XXXVII, 1679).

¹³St. Augustine in *Ps. XC enarr.* I, 9 (ML, XXXVII, 1157).

¹⁴St. Augustine in *Ps. LXXXV*, 5 (ML, XXXVII, 1083).

¹⁵A. Nygren, *Corpus Christi*, in *En Bok om Kyrkan, av Svenska teologer* (Lund, 1943), p. 20.

¹⁶St. Hilary in *Ps. CXXV*, 6 (ML, IX, 688).

¹⁷Karl Adam, *Das Wesen des Katholizismus*, 4 Ausgabe (1927), p. 24.

¹⁸See E. Mersch, S.J., *Le Corps Mystique du Christ, Etudes de Theologie Historique*, 2 vols., 2nd edition (Louvain 1936).

¹⁹The image of the Bride and her mystical marriage with Christ (Eph. v, 23f.) expresses the intimate union. Even the image of the House built of many stones, the corner stone being Christ (Eph. ii, 20f; cf. ɪ Pet. ii, 6), tends to the same purpose: many are becoming one, and the tower appears as it were built of one stone (cf. Hermans, *Shepherd*, Vis. III, ii, 6, 8). And again "the People of God" is to be regarded as an organic whole. There is no reason whatever to be troubled by the variety of vocabularies used. The main idea and contention is obviously the same in all cases.

²⁰Cf. George Florovsky, "The Catholicity of the Church", in this volume.

²¹Such as in Khomiakov or in Moehler's *Die Einheit in der Kirche*.

²²Cf. St. Augustine in *Evang. Joannis tract*, CXXIV, 5 (ML, XXXV, 19f., 7).

²³See Khomiakov's essay *On the Church;* English translation by W. J. Birkbeck, *Russia and the English Church* (first published 1895), ch. XXIII, pp. 193-222.

²⁴For a more detailed treatment, see George Florovsky, *The Antinomies of Christian History*, which will be published in the *Collected Works* of Georges Florovsky.

CHAPTER V

¹C. H. Turner, *Apostolic Succession*, in "Essays on the Early History of the Church and the Ministry," edited by H. B. Swete (London, 1918), pp. 101-102. See also Yves M. J. Congar, O.P., *La Tradition et les traditions, II. Essai Théologique* (Paris, 1963), pp. 21 ss.

²Cf. E. Flesseman-van-Leer, *Tradition and Scripture in the Early Church* (Assen, 1954), pp. 145-185; Damien van den Eynde, *Les Normes de l'Enseignment Chrétien dans la litterature patristique des trois premiers siècles* (Gembloux-Paris, 1933), pp. 197-212; J. K. Stirniman, *Die Praescriptio Tertullians im Lichte des römischen Rechts und der Theologie* (Freiburg, 1949); and also the introduction and notes of R. F. Refoulé, O.P., in the edition of De *praescriptione*, in the "Sources Chrétiennes," 46 (Paris, 1957).

³Cf. F. Kattenbusch, *Das Apostolische Symbol*, Bd. ɪɪ (Leipzig, 1900), ss. 30 ff., and also his note in the "Zeitschrift f. neutest. Theologie," x (1909), ss. 331-332.

⁴It has been contended that *charisma veritatis* was actually simply the Apostolic doctrine and the truth (of the Divine Revelation), so that St. Irenaeus did not imply any special ministerial endowment of the bishops.

See Karl Müller, *Kleine Beiträge zur alten Kirchengeschichte*, 3. Das *Charisma veritatis* und der Episcopat bei Irenaeus, in "Zeitschrift f. neut. Wissenschaft," Bd. xxiii (1924), ss. 216-222; cf. van den Eynde, pp. 183-187; Y. M.-J. Congar, O.P., *La Tradition et les traditions, Étude historique* (Paris, 1960), pp. 97-98; Hans Freiherr von Campenhausen, *Kirchliches Amt und geistliche Vollmacht in den ersten drei Jahrhudderten* (Tübingen, 1953), ss. 185 ff.; and also—with the special emphasis on the character of "Succession"—Einar Molland, *Irenaeus of Lugdunum and the Apostolic Succession*, in the "Journal of Ecclesiastical History," I.I, 1950, pp. 12-28, and *Le développement de l'idée de succession apostolique*, in the "Revue d'historie et de philosophie réligieuses," xxxiv.I, 1954, pp. 1-29. See, on the other hand, the critical remarks of Arnold Ehrhardt, *The Apostolic Succession in the first two centuries of the Church* (London, 1953), pp. 207-231, esp. 213-214.

⁵Cf. Dom Odo Casel, O.S.B., *Benedict von Nursia als Pneumatiker*, in "Heilige Überlieferung" (Münster, 1938), ss. 100-101: *Die heilige Überlieferung ist daher in der Kirche von Anfang an nicht bloss ein Weitergeben von Doktrinen nach spätjudischen (nachchristlicher) Art gewesen, sondern ein lebendiges Weiterblühen des göttlichen Lebens.* In a footnote Dom Casel sends the reader back to John Adam Möhler.

⁶G. L. Prestige, *Fathers and Heretics* (London, 1940), p. 43.

⁷Flesseman, pp. 92-96. On St. Irenaeus see Flesseman, 100-144; van den Eynde, 159-187; B. Reynders, Paradosis, *Le progrès de l'dée de tradition jusqu' à Saint Irénée*, in the "Recherches de théologie ancienne et mediévale," v (1933), 155-191; *La polemique de Saint Irénée, ibidem*, vii (1935), 5-27; Henri Holstein, *La Tradition des Apotres chez Saint Irénée*, in the "Recherches de Science réligieuse," xxxvi (1949), 229-270; *La Tradition dans l'Eglise* (Paris, 1960); André Benoit, *Ecriture et Tradition chez Saint Irénée*, in the "Révue d'histoire et de philosophie réligieuses," xl (1960), 32-43; *Saint Irénée, Introduction à l'étude de sa théologie* (Paris, 1960).

⁸See Guido Müller, *Lexicon Athanasianum, sub voce: id quod quis docendo, scribendo, credendo intendit.*

⁹See Karl Prächter, *Richtungen und Schulen im Neuplatonismus*, in "Genethliakon" (Carl Roberts zum 8. März 1910), (Berlin, 1910). Prächter translates σκοπὸς as *Zielpunct* or *Grundthema* (s. 128 f.). He characterizes the method of Jamblichos as an "universalistische Exegese" (138). Proclus, in his Commentary on Timaeus, contrasts Porphyry and Jamblichos: Porphyry interpreted texts μερικώτερον, while Jamblichos did it ἐποπτικώτερον, that is in a comprehensive or syntretic manner: in *Tim. I*, pp. 204, 24 ff., quoted by Prächter, s. 136.

¹⁰*Select Treatises of St. Athanasius*, freely translated by J. H. Cardinal Newman, Vol. II (Eighth impression, 1900), pp. 250-252.

¹¹H. E. W. Turner, *The Pattern of Christian Truth* (London, 1954), pp. 193-1944.

¹²C. R. B. Shapland rightly suggested that θεμέλιον in this text meant for St. Athanasius precisely the threefold Name as invoked in the Holy Baptism. In fact, St. Athanasius quotes the Dominical commission a bit later in the same section of his epistle and introduces it in this way: the Lord 'ordered them [the Apostles] to lay this foundation for the Church, saying' . . . The Apostles went, and so they taught: *The Letters of Saint Athanasius concerning the Holy Spirit*, translated with Introduction and

Notes by C. R. B. Shapland (London, 1951) p. 152, n. 2 (on p. 134).
¹³See Dom M. Capuyns, *L'origine des Capitula Pseudo-Celestiniens contre les Semipelagiens,* in 'Révue Bénédictine,' t. 41 (1929), pp. 156-170; especially Karl Federer, *Liturgie und Glaube, Eine theologiegeschichtliche Untersuchung* (Freiburg in der Schweiz, 1950) (=Paradosis, ɪv); cf. Dom B. Capelle, *Autorité de la liturgie chèz les Pères,* in 'Recherches de Théologie ancienne et médiévale,' t. xxɪ (1954), pp. 5-22.
¹³ J. N. D. Kelly, *Early Christian Creeds* (London, 1950), p. 167.
¹⁴See Federer, *op. cit.,* s. 59 ff.; F. De Pauw, *La justification des traditions non écrites chèz Tertullien,* in 'Ephemerides Theologicae Lovanienses,' t. xɪx, 1/2, 1942, pp. 5-46. Cf. also Georg Kretschmar, *Studien zur frühchristlichen Trinitätstheologie* (Tübingen, 1956).
¹⁵See his introduction to the edition of the treatise *De Spiritu Sancto* in 'Sources Chrétiennes,' (Paris, 1945), pp. 28 ss.
¹⁶See the valuable study by August Deneffe, S.J., *Dogma. Wort und Begriff,* in the 'Scholastik,' Jg. vɪ (1931), ss. 381-400 and 505-538.
¹⁷Cf. Hermann Dörries, *De Spiritu Sancto, Der Beitrag des Basilius zum Abschluss des trinitarischen Dogmas* (Göttingen, 1956); J. A. Jungmann, S.J., *Die Stellung Christi im liturgischen Gebet,* 2. Auflage (Münster i/W, 1962), ss. 155 ff., 163 ff.; Dom David Amand, *L'ascese monastique de Saint Basile,* Editions de Maredsous (1949), pp. 75-85. The footnotes in the critical editions of the treatise *De Spiritu S.* by C. F. H. Johnson (Oxford, 1892) and by Benoit Pruche, O.P. (in the 'Sources Chrétiennes,' Paris, 1945) are highly instructive and helpful. On *disciplina arcani* see O. Perler, s.v. Arkandisciplin, in 'Reallexikon für Antike und Christentum,' Bd. ɪ (Stuttgart, 1950), ss. 671-676. Joachim Jeremias, *Die Abendmahlsworte Jesu* (Göttingen, 1949), ss. 59 ff., 78 ff., contended that *disciplina arcani* could be detected already in the formation of the text of the Gospels, and actually existed also in Judaism; cf. the sharp criticism of this thesis by R. P. C. Hanson, *Tradition in the Early Church* (London, 1962), pp. 27 ss.
¹⁸Cf. German Mártil, O.D., *La tradición en San Agustín a través de la controversia pelagiana* (Madrid, 1942) (originally in 'Revista española de Teología,' Vol. ɪ, 1940, and ɪɪ, 1942); Wunibald Roetzer, *Des heiligen Augustinus Schriften als liturgie-geschichtliche Quelle* (München, 1930); see also the studies of Federer and Dom Capelle, as quoted above.
¹⁹Cf. Louis de Montadon, *Bible et Eglise dans l'Apologétique de Saint Augustin,* in the "Recherches de Science réligieuse," t. ɪɪ (1911), pp. 233-238; Pierre Battiffol, *Le Catholicisme de Saint Augustin,* 5th ed. (Paris, 1929), pp. 25-27 (see the whole chapter ɪ, L'Eglise règle de foi); and especially A. D. R. Polman, *The Word of God according to St. Augustine* (Grand Rapids, Michigan, 1961), pp. 198-208 (it is a revised translation of the book published in Dutch in 1955 — *De Theologie van Augustinus, Het Woord Gods bij Augustinus*); see also W. F. Dankbaar, *Schriftgezag en Kerkgezag bij Augustinus,* in the 'Nederlands Theologisch Tijdschrift,' xɪ (1956-1957), ss. 37-59 (the article is written in connection with the Dutch edition of Polman's book).

CHAPTER VI

[1]Dom Gregory Dix, "Jurisdiction, Episcopal and Papal, in the Early Church," *Laudate*, XVI (No. 62, June 1938), 108.

[2]Georg Kretschmar, "Die Konzile der Alten Kirche," in: *Die ökumenischen Konzile der Christenheit*, hg. v. H. J. Margull, Stuttgart (1961), p. 1.

[3]Dom Gregory Dix, *op. cit.*, p. 113.

[4]See Eduard Schwartz, "Über die Reichskonzilien von Theodosius bis Justinian" (1921), reprinted in his *Gesammelte Schriften*, IV (Berlin, 1960), pp. 111—158.

[5]Cf. my article, "Empire and Desert: Antinomies of Christian History", *The Greek Orthodox Theological Review*, III (No. 2, 1957), 133—159.

[6]See V. V. Bolotov, *Lectures on the History of the Ancient Church*, III (1913), p. 320 ff. (Russian), and his *Letters to A. A. Kireev*, ed. by D. N. Jakshich (1931), pp. 31 ff. (Russian); also A. P. Dobroklonsky, "The Ecumenical Councils of the Orthodox Church. Their Structure," *Bogoslovlje*, XI (2 & 3, 1936), 163—172 and 276—287. (Serbian.)

[7]Hans Küng, *Strukturen der Kirche*, 1962, pp. 11—74.

[8]Bolotov, *Lectures*, I (1907), pp. 9—14.

[9]Cf. Monald Goemans, O.F.M., *Het algemeene Concilie in de vierde eeuw* (Nijmegen-Utrecht, 1945).

[10]"Primauté des quatre premiers conciles oecuméniques", *Le Concile et les Conciles, Contribution à l'histoire de la vie conciliaive de l'Eglise* (1960), p. 75—109.

[11]For further discussion of this topic see my articles: "The Function of Tradition in the Ancient Church," *The Greek Orthodox Theological Review*, IX (No. 2, 1964), 181—200, and "Scripture and Tradition: An Orthodox point of view," *Dialog*, II (No. 4, 1963), 288—293. Cf. also "Revelation and Interpretation," in: *Biblical Authority for Today*, edited by Alan Richardson and W. Schweitzer (London and Philadelphia, 1951), pp. 163—180.

[12]See B. Reynders, "Paradosis, Le progrès de l'idée de tradition jusqu'à Saint Irénée," *Recherches de théologie ancienne et mediévale*, V (1933), 155—191, and "La polemique de Saint Irénée," *ibidem*, VII (1935), 5—27.

[13]Cf. P. Smulders, "Le mot et le concept de tradition chez les Pères," *Recherches de Science religieuse*, 40 (1952), 41—62, and Yves Congar, *La Tradition et les traditions, Etude historique* (Paris 1960), p. 57 ff.

[14]See, first of all, J. Fessler, *Institutiones Patrologiae*, denuo recensuit, auxit, edidit B. Jungmann, I (Innsbruck, 1890), pp. 15—57; E. Amann, "Pères de l'église," *Dictionnaire de Theologie Catholique*, XII, cc. 1192—1215; Basilius Steidle, O.S.B., "Heilige Vaterschaft," *Benedictinische Monatsschrift*, XIV (1932), 215—226; "Unsere Kirchenväter," *ibidem*, 387—398 and 454—466.

[15]Cf. Basilius Steidle, *Patrologia* (Friburgi Brisg., 1937), p. 9: *qui saltem aliquo tempore per vinculum fidei et caritatis Ecclesiae adhaeserunt testesque sunt veritatis catholicae.*

[16]G. L. Prestige, *Fathers and Heretics* (London, 1940), p. 8. Italics are mine.

[17]See Eusebius, *hist. eccl.*, V. 28.6, quoting an anonymous treatise, *Against the heresy of Artemon*, of the third century. The attribution of this treatise to Hippolytus is doubtful.

[18]See my article "Offenbarung, Philosophie und Theologie," *Zwischen den*

Zeiten, IX (1931), pp. 463—480. — Cf. Karl Adam, *Christus unser Bruder* (1926), p. 116 f.: *Der konservative Traditionsgeist der Kirche fliesst unmittelbar aus ihrer christozentrischen Grundhaltung. Von dieser Grundstellung aus wandte sich die Kirche von jeher gegen die Tyrannie von Führerpersönlichkeiten, von Schulen und Richtungen. Da, wo durch diese Schulen das christliche Bewusstsein, die überlieferte Botschaft von Christus, getrübt oder bedroht schien, da zögerte sie nicht, selbst über ihre grössten Söhne hinwegzuschreiten, über einen Origenes, Augustin, ja — hier und dort — selbst über einen Thomas von Aquin. Und überall da, wo grundsätzlich nicht die Überlieferung, nicht das Feststehen auf dem Boden der Geschichte, der urchristlichen Gegenbeit, der lebendigen fortdauernden Gemeinschaft, sondern die eigene Spekulation und das eigene kleine Erlebnis und das eigene arme Ich zum Träger der Christusbotschaft gemacht werden sollte, da sprach sie umgehend ihr Anathema aus ... Die Geschichte der kirchlichen Verkündigung ist nichts anderes als ein zähes Festhalten an Christus, eine folgestrenge Durchführung des Gebotes Christi: Nur einer sei eurer Lehrer, Christus.* — Actually, this pathetic passage is almost a paraphrase of the last chapter of the (first) *Commonitorium* of St. Vincent, in which he sharply discriminates between the common and universal mind of the Church and the *privatae opiniunculae* of individuals: *quidquid vero, quamquis ille sanctus et doctus, quamvis episcopus, quamvis confessor et martyr, praeter omnes aut etiam contra omnes senserit* (cap. XXVII).

CHAPTER VII

[1]It has been recently suggested that Gnostics were actually the first to invoke formally the authority of an "Apostolic Tradition" and that it was their usage which moved St. Irenaeus to elaborate his own conception of Tradition. D. B. Reynders, "Paradosis: Le progrès de l'idée de tradition jusqu'a Saint Irenee," in *Recherches de Théologie ancienne et medievale*, V (1933), Louvain, 155—191. In any case, Gnostics used to refer to "tradition."

[2]Paul Maas, ed., *Frühbyzantinische Kirchenpoesie*, I (Bonn, 1910), p. 24.

[3]Louis Bouyer, "Le renouveau des etudes patristiques," in *La Vie Intellectuelle*, XV (Fevrier 1947), 18.

[4]Mabillon, *Bernardi Opera, Praefatio generalis*, n. 23 (Migne, *P. L.*, CLXXXII, c. 26).

[5]Cf. M. Lot-Borodine, "La doctrine de la deification dans l'Eglise grecque jusqu'au XI siecle," in *Revue de l'histoire des religions*, tome CV, Nr 1 (Janvier-Fevrier 1932), 5—43; tome CVI, Nr 2/3 (Septembre-Decembre 1932), 525—74; tome CVII, Nr 1 (Janvier-Fevrier 1933), 8—55.